MIRACLE DOGS

ADVENTURES ON WHEELS

SANDY JOHNSON

PUBLISHED BY FASTPENCIL

Published by FastPencil
307 Orchard City Drive
Suite 210
Campbell CA 95008 USA
info@fastpencil.com
(408) 540-7571
(408) 540-7572 (Fax)
http://www.fastpencil.com

These stories are based on facts as told by the subjects to Sandy Johnson.

Printed in the United States of America.

First Edition

FOR CHARLEY

❧

Acknowledgments

I wish to thank those who told their stories of love and loyalty and enduring bonds with their pets: TJ Jordi; Andy Dennis & Susan Hollar; Amy Boswell; Elizabeth Jacobson; Curtiss Lindsay; Michele Marshall; Michael Baines; Andrea Stewart; Bany Alivi-Alipour; Michele Pinto; Beverly Dennis; Matt Pike; Lucy Wang and Xaioli.

My thanks to Annie Tucker for her great editing, and to Brooke Warner for her advice. I am indebted to Lisa-Marie Mulkern at HandicappedPets.com for contacting the pet owners and providing me with their information.

My continuing thanks to Chris Rungé of Chris's Critter Sitters for keeping Charley happy and busy during my writing hours.

Lastly, and mostly, I am grateful to my son Mark C. Robinson, founder and president of HandicappedPets.com who invented the miraculous Walkin' Wheels dog wheelchair, and invited me to write these stories. I am forever honored to get to know these extraordinary pets and their heroic owners.

CONTENTS

PROLOGUE: THE DOG WHEELCHAIR IN A CHANGING WORLD

As I write this, I am flying on Air India from Osaka, Japan, to Hong Kong. They just served lunch. The smell of curry is in the air, the woman beside me brought her own chopsticks, a flight attendant is wearing a hijab (Muslim head covering), and the Japanese businessman across the aisle just handed me his business card with two hands as he bowed in his seat. It's as if someone put the world's cultures into a dice cup, shook them up, and rolled them down my airplane's aisle.

My name is Mark C. Robinson. I'm the inventor of the Walkin' Wheels dog wheelchair. My mission for this trip is to support my friends in Asia who are trying to help elderly, disabled, and handicapped dogs live happy, healthy lives.

My trip, starting in China, has been filled with wide-eyed amazement as I've handed people my business card, featuring a picture of a dog in a wheelchair. Usually, the conversation begins with me trying to tell them in Chinese what I do. *Go luan ee*, with the proper singsong tones, means "dog wheelchair," but it sounds like nonsense to them, so they assume, rightfully, that it's my fledgling Chinese and I'm trying to say something completely different. But as we talk further and I show them my business card, they get the idea. It doesn't take long for them to realize that it is an idea with possibilities.

My meeting in Beijing with Together for Animals in China, an advocacy group whose tagline is "Dogs are friends, not food," was the most productive. One of the members cares for Wang Wang, a dog in a wheelchair who elicits stares, laughs, compassion, and curiosity whenever she rolls along. This group, with strong connections throughout animal shelters and the hospital community in China, is getting the word out with pamphlets, brochures, and websites.

There are a few people in China who make dog wheelchairs, but they are poorly made. Because they are not flexible and adjustable, they fit only one dog and cannot be reused again and again, like Walkin' Wheels. The Chinese people care about this kind of efficiency and utility. They are excited to have a source for quality products.

As China's wealth increases, people with more disposable income are able to afford to own and care for a dog. When their dog can no longer walk because of old age, illness, or injury, families are faced with the decision to end the dog's life or use a wheelchair. They make the same decision that you or I would make—if they know that a dog wheelchair exists. China's middle class, a strong and growing element of Chinese society, is taking notice.

Another stop along my journey was in Hong Kong, where GTO Limited, an international trading company, has begun successfully distributing the product in Hong Kong. Hong Kong is already filled with dog lovers. Demand is increasing here as people learn about the product. GTO works through veterinarians, trade shows, articles in the news, advertisements, and its popular website. It won't be long before a dog in a wheelchair on the street or in the park will be a common sight in Kowloon.

A darker note came during a Skype call with my distributor in Iran. Many years ago, before the embargo, we sold a few dog wheelchairs there. Unfortunately, the religious leaders have passed a law that if a dog is seen on the street, it should be shot and the owner arrested. This is in part, from what I understand, because owning dogs is a "Western affectation" that these leaders don't want spreading in their country. Also, a dog is considered dirty or taboo in their religion. It is possible that we may begin selling again if the embargo lifts. This underground connection between the dog lovers of Iran and the rest of the world is one we need to foster.

My stop in Japan was a wonderful treat. People in Japan know a lot about dog wheelchairs, and the distributor there, Handicapped-Dogs.jp, is highly successful. It loves its dogs and is quick to provide the care and equipment they need. The owner of the company, Marty, and I toured Kyoto, handing out business cards and speaking about the products. People's faces lit up in delight as they saw the photos.

I was not able to visit all my distributors; Singapore, Malaysia, South Korea, Israel, and Australia will have to wait until my next trip. But as more and more people around the world are introduced to the possibility that they can support their best friends when they can no longer walk, the magic of Walkin' Wheels spreads. It is easy to see the love and kindness this idea inspires.

But it's the stories that seem to matter the most. My work is filled with stories of heroic dogs and people who would not give up—stories of health, healing, and hope. There are miraculous rescues, courageous recoveries, and perfectly healthy dogs in wheelchairs—stories that want to be told. My mom's a writer—I think I'll ask her if she wants to write them.

Another quick stop in Hong Kong, and it's back home to Amherst, New Hampshire, where the great people at HandicappedPets.com have been helping people around the world get the products, services, and support they need to help dogs live long, happy, healthy lives.

Mark C. Robinson

Introduction: Charley and the Coyote

Charley is my six-year-old, twelve-pound, black female Brussels Griffon. She has large, expressive eyes, a monkey face, and the will and determination of a three-hundred-pound lioness. I call her my "familiar," a term used in ancient folklore to describe the bond between a witch and her special animal—usually a cat or a dog—who assists her in her practice of witchcraft. But since I possess no such gifts, I mean it to describe the steadfast companionship between Charley and me that began on the day I first set eyes on her, an eight-week-old ball of fur with a fully formed personality.

She became my muse, curled beside me as I dreamed my stories and carved them with my pen onto the pages of my notebook. It was only when I tapped them out on my laptop that Charley got bored and wanted to play or go out. Apparently, she did not consider tapping on a keyboard real writing.

On this fine September morning, Charley and I were out for our usual morning walk—seven fifteen, to be exact—along our quiet, leafy street at the foothills of Griffith Park in Los Angeles. As usual, Charley was making her frequent stops to sniff the bushes to see who had been there before us. I call it her message board. Sometimes she leaves a message of her own. (*For a good time, call Charley?*)

I was standing on the sidewalk not more than a foot from where she had decided to squat, when suddenly it appeared—a large, mangy coyote with murder in his eyes. In a flash, Charley was off the ground and in the coyote's jaws.

I have to slow the action down in my mind, frame by frame, to tell the story. What followed involved no thought, only pure instinct. The leash still in my hand, I let out a loud, animal-like scream and pulled hard at the leash, reeling it in toward me until I was close to the coyote, so close I could see the blood dripping from his teeth, and pulling so hard that in retrospect I'm surprised I didn't break Charley's neck or strangle her.

I don't know if it was my screams or my furious pulling on the leash, but, incredibly, the coyote gave up and released her. I say "incredibly" because the vet told me said she'd never heard of a coyote giving up once he had his prey in his jaws. She was amazed, too, that the coyote didn't turn and attack me. Which is what he was going to have to do before I'd let him kill a member of my family.

The surgery lasted hours. The vet explained that the wounds were a hair's breadth from piercing both Charley's chest wall and her abdominal wall, either of which would have meant instant death. "That was very courageous of you to fight him off," she said, looking at the cuts the leash made on both my hands.

I looked at her. Courage was not at issue.

Weeks later, when Charley's sutures had healed and the nightmares began to fade, I began to see it as a battle between the coyote, known in many cultures as the Trickster, and my spiritual familiar, played out before me and calling me into battle. We were both warriors, Charley and I, and we triumphed.

At the time I accepted the invitation to write the stories in this book about disabled dogs spared euthanasia by the dedication and resourcefulness of their owners, I had no idea how deep that dedication ran, or how transcendent their commitment. It was only when my own Charley's life hung in the balance did I see with absolute clarity the depth of the connection between pet owners and their four-legged family members.

And I learned something about community, too. I live in a high-rise apartment building, and with a few exceptions (I am a displaced New Yorker), I've never bothered to get to know my neighbors beyond "Good morning, lovely day." But word spread quickly about the attack, and suddenly people I barely recognized were stopping to express their shock and concern. Charley was suddenly a hero. We could hardly make it down the street without stopping to "sign autographs."

My newfound understanding about the power of our shared connection with our pets opened my eyes—and my heart—to the many miracles that are the inspiration for this book.

Sandy Johnson

1

Scooter's Story: TJ and Me Forever

"Any man with money to make the purchase may become a dog's owner. But no man—spend he ever so much coin and food and tact in the effort—may become a dog's Master without consent of the dog. Do you get the difference? And he whom a dog once unreservedly accepts as Master is forever that dog's God."

—Albert Payson Terhune, *Lad: A Dog*

This is the story of two souls, one four-legged, the other two-legged, who were meant to meet and fulfill their shared destiny. First, Scooter's story:

A very cold day in February 2011. I was crouched on the side of the road, hiding from the people and noises coming from the street. Most of all, I was hiding from the man who shot me, my owner. I was a growing puppy, six months old and always hungry; they didn't want me anymore because they couldn't feed me, so they turned me out of the house and chased me away. Lost, alone, and hungry, I wandered for days. Finally, I gave up and went home, hoping they would take me back.

But when I showed up at their door, the big man took down his rifle and shot me. I turned and ran, but he shot me two more times, once in each flank, and once in the back. I tried to keep on running, but I could move only as fast as my two front legs would carry me. When I couldn't move anymore, I hid in the bushes.

I don't know how long I had been lying there when some people spotted me and stopped their car and tried to pick me up. I was frightened at first and tried to get away from them, but I had no strength left. They put me in a big blue plastic tub in the back of their car and talked about taking me someplace where I could be "put to sleep."

They drove to a building where many dogs were barking and lots of people were coming and going. A man came out and opened the back of the car and looked at me. Gently, he opened my mouth and looked at my teeth and ears, and then he scratched the top of my head and picked me up and carried me into the building. The smell of dogs and cats and critters of every sort filled the air. I heard the people who picked me up say, "We think he was hit by a car .... Better put him to sleep .... Poor doggie .... "

The nice man took me into a room and put me on a big steel table with a towel on it to keep me warm. He looked at my eyes, my ears, and my mouth again. Then he looked at my back legs. Carefully, he picked me up and put me on the floor and walked a short distance away and turned to me. Using my front legs, I scooted along the smooth floor, which was so much easier than rocks and grass, and came to him. He turned and walked away again, and I followed him. He chuckled and said I was a real scooter. I liked the man; I liked the way he looked into my eyes and smiled as if we were old friends. I followed him around the table a few more times before he stopped and scratched me on the top of the head again and then under my neck. I just melted into him from that moment.

He picked up the phone. His expression was discouraging; he wasn't liking whatever it was he was hearing. When he put the phone down, he got up and spoke to the people who brought me in—"He's got great character ...

gets around on his own … "—and then they wandered off into another room.

Before long, someone brought in big bowls of food and water, which I finished off three times, until I couldn't eat anymore. I curled up on a blanket on the floor and fell asleep.

After a while, the man came back in with a towel that he wrapped around me. I didn't know what was happening, but I remembered the conversation about being "put to sleep." I tried to get away, but the more I wriggled, the tighter his grip got. Now I was scared.

He had covered me up completely with the towel, including my eyes, and went through a couple of doors, and it got really cold. *This must be the end*, I thought.

But then it got really warm. We were in the nice man's car. He talked to me for a long time. I couldn't understand all the words, but I could understand what he meant. We were friends; I had nothing to fear anymore. He drove for a while and then stopped at a bigger building. He grabbed that really big, warm blanket and some of the towels and took me inside. There were more dogs in there; they all came up and sniffed at me. Then I had my first bath.

The other dogs wouldn't leave me alone, I growled and snapped at them; it was all I could do, because I couldn't run. But then the nice man, my friend, came back in and showed me that the other dogs were not going to hurt me. For a long time, he stayed right next to me.

Finally, I got so tired that I just lay down and fell asleep. I know at some point he picked me up and carried me to another room and put me on a warm, comfy blanket.

When I woke up, I looked around for my new friend, only to discover that he was right next to me, with his arm over my back. I licked his face for the longest time. Then he got up and brought me another bowl of food.

After a couple of days lying around, he took me back to that place with that big steel table, but for some reason, now I wasn't worried. I had learned his name was TJ and that we would be friends forever.

TJ came out of another room with a big box in his hands and took out a bunch of strange-looking things and some tools and got busy. When he was finished, he picked me up and took me over to the thing with wheels that he had been putting together. After getting my back legs into the strange-looking contraption, TJ put me down on the floor and wrapped the thing around me and snapped it on.

I just looked up at him, wondering what he wanted me to do. TJ grabbed onto my collar and pulled on me … and suddenly I could move! With ease! I could even run again, I was still really fast, I ran everywhere I could reach. I could hear people behind me laughing, but I didn't care … *I could run again!* I ran and I ran, and I ran till I couldn't run anymore. Finally, I got really tired and fell asleep underneath TJ's desk while still in the contraption. I felt so good.

When I finally woke up, I made the biggest decision of my life: I decided to adopt my best friend, TJ.

TJ's Story

The dog, a six-month-old Border Collie, was brought in from the back of a beat-up hatchback inside a blue con-

tainer. He was a sad sight—a heart-wrenching puppy, not
even a teenager. His hind legs and hips were scraped from
scooting on the ground. Unfortunately, I knew we
couldn't afford to take him for X-rays, not on our government budget. But when I looked him in the eyes, we con-
nected. It was like a total alignment of all the planets in the
universe, an almost audible *ping*. I knew right then that I
was going to try—try anything.

We brought him in and carried him to the treatment
room, where the table was set up to euthanize him. I put
him down on the table and looked at those pathetic, with-
ered legs, and my heart dropped. There were no signs of
new or fresh injuries. I tousled his head, and he smiled
back at me. I set him down and backed up, hoping for a
miracle, a sign, anything.

I hadn't gotten two steps away before he screamed. It
wasn't a yelp of pain or a howl of sorrow. It was a sudden,
soul-stopping scream that cried, *Don't leave me!* The
scream was unlike anything I'd ever heard before; it was
enough to stop me in my tracks.

He had pulled himself along, his useless legs dragging
behind him as he scooted toward me. Ecstatic that I had
stopped, he dragged himself over to me and sat at my feet.
His head was cocked back, and his tongue was lolling. I
looked into his eyes, and I knew that, no matter what, I
had to find a way to help him.

I started around the table, and he followed, screaming
joyously and sliding along the floor. To think that he had
been dragging himself like this through streets and woods
and rocks made me cringe. We started to chase each other

around the room like two little boys, me laughing and his tail wagging.

I had to stop and call the vet. I needed to know the next step; I had to know if there were any other options available for him. When the vet listened to his story, she explained that even without an X-ray, it was clear that the dog was paralyzed, and probably had been so for a while. His scream was most likely his only defense when, stranded and alone, predators were near. The fear I felt for him at this past danger, together with the joy that he had survived, carved itself into my heart. This dog was meant to be saved. Regretfully, she suggested that it might be kinder to put him down. Impressed as she was with his survival, quality of life in the shelter would be poor, and finding someone to take care of him would be nearly impossible. I hung up the phone, my mood bleak.

But I was not hopeless. I called the director. I always valued her opinion on such matters. She knew the budget issues, the risk involved, and the very small chance of his ever finding either a rescue or an adopter. She also realized that the fact of his survival so far was a miracle. Still, with apology ringing in her voice, she agreed with the vet's suggestion. I was devastated. I couldn't accept it. I didn't know the scope of issues that Scooter (by then I had named him) brought with him, but I knew that I would go through hell before I gave up on him. I had to save him.

At that moment, Scooter was mine. Or, rather, I was his. In my heart, I knew that losing him, even after knowing him for only an hour, would wound me more deeply than I could stand. At that moment I took him on, took him in, and opened my world to one of the greatest loves I will ever know. This pillow-stealing, wheelchair-breaking, run-you-down-and-make-you-glad, oversize dust mop has become one of my best friends.

TJ Jordi, firefighter, certified master diver, service dog trainer, and recipient of the Humane Heroes Award, is now the director of Tennessee's Cheatham County Animal. With the support of a small but dedicated staff and rescue network, they have not had to euthanize a single healthy, adoptable animal in three years.

Scooter has become a celebrity. He was the grand marshal of the Cheatham County Special Olympics in 2012 and 2013, and won a bronze medal in 2012 and a gold medal in 2013. He is being trained as a therapy dog for people in wheelchairs, and he's been to nearly all the schools in Cheatham County and has served as the lead dog in all Cheatham County Christmas Parades since his arrival. He is proof that handicapped pets can live full and productive lives.

Together, TJ and Scooter are fulfilling the destiny that brought them together.

Learn more about Scooter and the other pets and people in this book. See color photos, more stories, and upload your own at HandicappedPets.com/MiracleDogs [http://handicappedpets.com/MiracleDogs]

2

DUKE'S STORY: STRAY NO MORE

The street will never truly be home. Long ago the dog began a journey of no return when it started down the road with man. The street dog wanders, yet it hasn't strayed; ever loyal, it lingers on the periphery of affection; alone it wanders, eager to rejoin the pack, where it really belongs. Man's lost friend is waiting to come home.

—*Street Dogs of South Central,* a film by Bill Marin

Andy Dennis is passionate about strays. Whether he is driving or on foot, when he spots a stray on the street, he pulls over to see if the dog has a collar; if it doesn't, Andy sets about finding the dog a home. He lives in Des Moines, Iowa, with his wife and four dogs, three of them former strays (the city of Des Moines does not permit more than four dogs in any one home). The fourth was his father's.

One evening on his way home from the auto shop where he works as a mechanic, Andy spotted a handsome brown dog—a Ridgeback, possibly, or a Boxer—wandering around a food-processing plant not far from where Andy lives. The dog was large but thin, obviously a stray. He had probably been drawn to the plant by the smell of food and had found a way in through a hole in the fence. Andy went home to get some food, left it just inside the fence, and waited. When the dog showed up, Andy tried to approach him, but the poor animal was too fearful. Instead, every night at the same time, Andy left the food in the same spot. It took weeks, but eventually the dog let

Andy pet him for a few minutes before the animal headed off into the nearby woods. Andy named him Duke.

When the plant's manager noticed and came out to confront Andy, Andy explained the dog's plight. The manager agreed to let the dog come around, since he did keep away rodents, and said that yes, it would be all right for Andy to come inside the fence to feed him.

This routine went on for months, but then, one frigid January day, a workman chased Duke away and told Andy not to come back. Andy argued that the manager had given his permission; the man told him that that manager was no longer there, and the new manager did not want the dog hanging around. The next day, the fence was repaired and locks were put on the gate.

The snows came. Andy, spotting Duke's tracks, continued to put the food out in a spot near but not too close to the plant. One night at about six thirty, Andy, seeing that the food had not been eaten and finding no fresh tracks, got into his car to look for Duke. As he headed down one of the back roads in the woods that led to the river, he saw a man with a rifle get into his truck and drive off. Suspicious, Andy wrote down the license plate number.

The next afternoon at about four thirty, two young women were standing on the riverbank, trying to capture photographs of eagles, when suddenly they heard sounds of heavy splashing coming from downriver. Training their lenses on the source of the commotion, they saw a dog desperately flailing in the near-freezing water. They ran along the bank, calling to him. Finally, they got the dog to head toward them, and they managed to pull him out. Covering the dog with their coats, the women put in a frantic call to Animal Control.

Andy, convinced something terrible had happened to Duke, drove down the same back road that led to the river where he'd seen the man with a rifle. As he approached, he saw Animal Control vehicles and officers carrying a big white blanket. Two young women, looking distressed, stood watching. Andy's heart sank. He jumped out of his car and rushed to them.

"Is that a dog in there?"

"Yes. These two girls found the dog in the river. He's still alive, but he can't walk." The officer opened the blanket. "An injury to his back. Is the dog yours?"

Andy explained that he had been feeding the dog and checking on him for months.

Andy followed the vehicle back to the Animal Rescue League of Iowa and asked to be allowed in. Upon examination, the vet found a wound from a .22-caliber shotgun and removed the bullet and metal fragments that were lodged in Duke's spine. "Technically," he said, "this dog should be put down."

Andy begged and pleaded, explained how much Duke had been through. He told them how much he had come to care for him and promised he would find Duke a home. Finally, Tom Colvin, the director, gave in. "There will be an investigation," he said.

Andy met with the detective assigned to the case. He described the man with the rifle and the truck he was driving and gave the detective the license plate number.

The detective tracked the man down and interviewed him but was unable to prove him guilty. A $6,000 reward was posted, funded by contributions from the Humane Society of the United States and the Animal Rescue League of Iowa.

Every day on his lunch break, Andy would come to see Duke, crawling into his cage to sit with him and comfort him. And, still certain that he had the right man, Andy began to follow him evenings, to spy on him. The man soon caught on and raced away the minute he spotted Andy. It was the same truck Andy had spotted before—a Chevy Blazer—but the plates didn't match. Since the man worked at the food-processing plant, Andy suspected the manager might have told the workman to find the dog and shoot him, and that the man might have then switched license plates when he realized he was being followed.

Duke was taken to the veterinary hospital at Iowa State University, where he underwent surgery to fuse his spine and remove the metal fragments from it. According to breed testing, he was found to be part Boxer and part American Staffordshire Terrier.

The two young women who found Duke in the river volunteered to adopt him. Another woman, Susan Hollar, who had seen Duke's story on Facebook, also applied. "I couldn't believe no one had adopted him after two or three weeks," Susan said, "so I started checking into whether it was something that I could do. Tom Colvin, executive director of the Animal Rescue League of Iowa, told me that they'd thought they had someone lined up to take Duke, but that had fallen through. I went up to the

Iowa State University Small Animal Hospital, where Duke was recovering, to get a look at him. I knew I wanted him."

Actually, the Animal Rescue League had received hundreds of calls offering to adopt the wounded dog, but Tom Colvin felt that Duke still had a long road to recovery. His back legs were paralyzed from the gunshot wound, and he would require a good deal of special care—including needing to be manually expressed to urinate. Also, the ARL wanted someone who had a handicapped-accessible home, few or no stairs, and the time to take care of Duke. Although Susan had a full-time job and was single, with two Lhasa Apsos, she thought it was something she could handle. She was selected to adopt Duke.

She had to be taught how to express his bladder and how to load him into his Walkin' Wheels dog wheelchair, donated by HandicappedPets.com. But she would have to carry him up and down stairs.

"In the beginning," Susan explains, "I was excited but a bit nervous. I had never cared for a 'special' dog before, and I had to make sure he remained in good health. I also had to make sure all three dogs were happy and got along. Because Duke had been out on his own for so long and he was not used to being around other dogs, I was worried he would feel he had to fight for food. It took some training to get him adjusted to home-family life, but after a time, everything became routine and we became a family.

"Today Duke has 3,400 Facebook friends, who follow him daily. He is a sweetheart—and an inspiration. He wheels around like a pro in his forever home."

Andy Dennis goes weekly to visit Duke and take him for walks in his wheels.

The man who shot Duke is still at large, but Andy is certain that one day he'll slip up and get caught. The reward for his arrest is now $6,500.

3

PUDDY'S STORY: DANCING ON WHEELS

"After years of having a dog, you know him. You know the meaning of his snuffs and grunts and barks. Every twitch of the ears is a question or statement, every wag of the tail is an exclamation."

–Robert R. McCammon, Boy's Life

Amy Boswell and her husband, Jason, live in Cass County, Missouri, about thirty minutes south of Kansas City, in a house on two wooded acres. Both animal lovers, they began to acquire dogs as soon as they were married. First there were two Basset Hounds, Daisy and Divot, adopted from their local shelter; then, four months after both Daisy and Divot had passed away, a picture of Puddy appeared on the 4 The Hounds Basset Rescue website, and immediately Amy fell in love. Puddy, a two-year-old male, fit right in, playing with their other Basset, Boomer. Soon after, Amy found a female Beagle wandering the streets, and after weeks of not being able to locate the dog's owners, she became part of the pack, too.

On a soft April morning, Amy was walking all three dogs around her backyard. Puddy lagged behind—not unusual for a "smell hound"—and Amy turned to coax him along. But as he walked up to her, Amy saw that he was dragging his back left toes. At first she thought he'd stepped on a thorn or maybe a pebble was lodged in his paw, but she checked and didn't find anything.

As Puddy walked on, his hips began to sway, subtly at first; then he started to stagger like he was drunk. A moment later, his whole back end, hips and legs, began to wobble, and his right leg started dragging. He was unable to pick up his toes. When he tried to squat, he nearly fell over. Amy was baffled. His eyes were bright and clear, and his tail was wagging; he was showing no signs of pain, yet this was obviously some kind of medical emergency. Her immediate thought was that Puddy was having a stroke. She hurried to get all the dogs inside the house so she could call the vet.

The vet told her to bring Puddy in immediately. She tried calling Puddy to get in the car, but by that time he was not able to use his right leg at all. "Puddy did not seem to know anything was wrong; he was just happy to be going for a ride."

The doctor injected his spine with medication and kept him overnight. The next morning, he called Amy to say Puddy was no better, perhaps a tad worse. Amy promptly got the dog to a neurologist.

"On the drive over, I called my husband, Jason, who was out of town on business that week, and told him I was on my way to the doggie ER, and that this was going to be expensive. I burst into tears and asked if I could please spend a few thousand dollars on my dog. I was pretty sure we could be facing a $3,000-plus vet bill. We are not wealthy by any means, but we did have some money set aside. We'd been saving money for trips to Switzerland, Paris, and Alaska. Choking through my tears, I told him that I would give up the trips to save my dog. Jason assured me we would do whatever we have to for Puddy.

"As I sat in the waiting room, I could not stop the tears. I was afraid I would lose my 'baby.' Puddy sat close, wagging his tail at me and tossing his big paw on my arm. I sank onto the floor so I could hug him while we waited.

"By the time our name was called, Puddy could no longer support himself to walk. He was paralyzed on the right side, and now the left leg was nearly useless. The techs brought out a sling. I tried to keep it together, but I was watching Puddy deteriorate in front of my eyes. Still, his tail wagged.

"The options were to do nothing and see if he might improve with time and rest, or to send him immediately into surgery. Since he had not improved overnight, even with the stabilizing injection, I opted for surgery, which gave him an 80 percent chance of a full recovery.

"By two o'clock that afternoon, surgery was done. The doctor said when they opened him up, to everyone's surprise and dismay, they found a massive disc material, which had blown out and bruised the spine. Now there was only a 50 percent chance of a full recovery. The doctor told me that Puddy was awake and wagging his tail so hard it was thudding against the sides of his kennel. I just wanted him home.

"The recovery was rough, with many complications and setbacks—until finally one day he busted out of his enclosure, and we knew he was feeling better. We got a sling in order to take him out for short potty walks. We tried 'dragging,' as the doctor suggested (allowing his back legs to drag along on the grass or other soft surfaces to bombard his spine with nerve signals to pick up his feet), and considered a wheelchair. But we decided that we would not get one so long as Puddy continued to improve.

"He was nearly 100 percent back to normal, when, nearly six months later to the day, Puddy started showing all the signs of a second disc blowout. He was now paralyzed in both back legs. This time, however, Puddy was not a candidate for a second surgery, since he had not recovered fully from the prior surgery. We decided then that we needed to get him a wheelchair.

"We wanted to give Puddy as much mobility as possible, and we could not continue to sling him as a permanent solution, so we carefully researched all the canine carts available and decided on the Walkin' Wheels. It took Puddy several weeks to get the hang of using the cart. At first, if the wheels so much as brushed a clump of grass or rolled over a pebble, he would come to a stop. But now he bulldozes right through bushes and brush, over rocks and tree limbs! When he sees us grab for the cart, his tail wags and he gets very excited. He is even slowly regaining some muscle movement in his thighs and his left leg.

"Thanks to his Walkin' Wheels, Puddy is back to being able to walk along with our other dogs and be a part of the pack; he can run and chase with the neighbor dogs and kids, and he has more freedom to explore, and he can once again resume being a stubborn, ground-sniffing hound. People, kids and adults alike, ask, 'How does he poop in that?' We simply say, 'You ever see a horse pulling a carriage or wagon? That's how.'

"There was *never* any doubt that Puddy would remain part of our family, disabled or not. With the Walkin' Wheels, he can once again be feisty and play with the other dogs (we have to reassure people he's not going to break), and he can still 'dance' for a cookie. Puddy's favorite activities are (still) snuggling on the couch, and chasing bicycles. I missed that little sashay. I'm so happy he has it back."

4

Thelma Louise; a Goat's Story: Not Just for Dogs

"You can judge a man's true character by the way he treats his fellow animals."

— *Paul McCartney*

Tucked away in the northwest corner of Ohio, over-looking Lake Erie and situated on what was once the Native American trail used by early westbound pioneers, is a small piece of paradise for all creatures large and small that might otherwise be put down. It is called Storybook Acres Disabled Animal Rescue.

The executive and founder is sixty-four-year-old retired medical legal consultant Michele Marshall, who has devoted her life to farm animals with disabilities. In 2001, she and her husband, Alan, took over an empty ten-acre farm in Conneaut, with one barn hardly big enough to hold a single lawn mower.

Shirley, a disabled goat unable to walk, was their first rescue. Alan figured out a way to make braces for Shirley's legs out of plastic pipe cut in half. Then they put bright red shoes on her feet and taught her to walk.

She was the first of many: dogs of all breeds, cats, birds, pigs, sheep, horses. At last count, there were thirty-two farm animals at Storybook Acres. "They were coming to us from all around the country with congenital joint deformities, shattered bones, blindness, deafness, and emotional scars. We give them medical care, rehabilitation, and a safe environment. The animals are all free to roam; they're never put in stalls, tied, or caged."

Now, Storybook Acres boasts three barns, a gift shop, a clinic, an exercise yard, a whirlpool, and an entire rehab facility.

When Alan decided they needed a guard dog, Michele brought home a Beagle that she found sitting under a tree at a garage sale. Never mind that he was blind and deaf—the dog needed a home.

Then along came Thelma Louise, a six-month-old goat with a broken ankle and suffering from brittle-bone disease. A farmer had called to say he was about to put her down. Michele wasted no time; she went to get her and brought her home to Storybook Acres. Although Thelma

played with the other goats during the day, at night she
was lonely and began to cry.

"One August day, a phone call came that a baby goat
was suffering and needed immediate care. I brought Annie
to the farm. She was so congested that she could not suck
on a bottle and was so weak she could not stand. We cared
for Annie in the house, keeping her warm and feeding her
with an eyedropper. Each night, Thelma would come in
and spend time with Annie, and they bonded. By the time
Annie was strong enough to suck, Thelma began pro-
ducing milk to feed her."

One of Michele's charges was Joshua, a very young
lamb weighing only three pounds, whose brain stem and
heart valve had not developed. He could neither sit nor
stand and had to be carried everywhere. Michele searched
the Internet for ideas on how to help animals with diffi-
culty walking and found a website, HandicappedPets.com,
in New Hampshire that designed dog wheelchairs that
could adjust to any size dog. Michele wondered just how
adjustable this might actually be. Could it be small enough
to help a baby lamb walk and then be resized as he grew to
adulthood? The website suggested that the Walkin'
Wheels brand might be able to do just that. A phone call
verified that it would indeed work.

"When little Joshua died, I asked them if the wheelchair
could be adjusted to fit Thelma. They explained that all
we needed to do was snap in a new set of larger wheels.

"I thought we would have to work with Thelma a lot
longer to get her used to the Walkin' Wheels, so I worked
with her first inside the clinic. But the moment I took her

outside, she ran straight over to a pear tree and began eating leaves. We could not keep up with her!

"She can turn on a dime in that wheelchair and just loves it. She had been walking on artificial legs since birth and would get so tired that going out to the pasture became more and more difficult. Now, she can go out into the pasture and outrun everyone on the farm.

"We have a goat that has artificial legs, and I am going to see if I can train her to use it. It's hard for her to walk around the pasture anymore, because she is very old. I'm hoping this spring will be easier for her. We also have a twenty-year-old Shepherd that doesn't get to go out in the pasture anymore because she gets too tired. I'm trying to get her to use the wheelchair, too, so that when the weather turns she can go out with me to the pasture.

"My mission is to let people understand that farm animals have so much to offer, and as long as they are happy, they should have that chance to live."

5

FROM IRAN: OMID THE MIRACLE DOG

"Of course I took it gently up
And brought it to my wife
Who loves all dogs, and now that pup
Shares in our happy life."
    —Robert William Service, "Abandoned Dog"

My ear has been cut, my body is filled with wounds, scars, and sores, my back legs don't work.... I stand tall, I stand strong, and I will never let anyone get me down. I am Omid.

Miracle Dog was what the veterinarian called him when he examined the German Shepherd mix just after he was rescued. The dog had been living on the streets of Iran for years, feeding on scraps of food wherever he could find them. Until the day in the winter of 2011 when he was run down by a car and left to die at the side of the road.

A man driving to his office saw the injured dog lying there and, for a brief moment, made eye contact with him. But he drove on. All the rest of that day, the man was haunted by the image of that dog and the expression in his eyes; he couldn't get it out of his mind. Finally, he called his driver and instructed him to go find the dog and bring him to the office. An hour later he arrived, and the man took the dog to the animal hospital.

After a thorough examination, the veterinarian told the man, Mohsen, the dog's spine was broken, his hind legs were paralyzed, and his ear was bleeding from where it had been cut. And there were burns on the back of his tail from having been dragged—by a motorcycle, the vet guessed.

The damage was too severe and beyond repair. The dog should be put out of his misery.

But Mohsen, deciding there must be a reason the dog had been put in his path, would not let him be euthanized; instead, he took him to VAFA, one of Iran's only dog shelters, where a volunteer began a social media campaign aimed at finding Omid a home. His photo and story on Facebook caught the eye of an Iranian woman living in France, who decided to sponsor the dog and pay his expenses to fly him out of Iran to America, to Washington, DC. She gave him the name Omid, meaning "hope." An American couple, founders of the nonprofit organization Street Dogs International, fostered him.

Another Iranian woman living in DC, Bany Alavi-Alipour, had been carefully following Omid's story, writing letters about the dog's desperate situation, and posting comments on Facebook. When Mohsen got word of Omid's rescue, he wrote a letter to Bany:

Every day I hoped for a miracle and good news about him, until on the first day of spring I heard that he was headed for America. I cried for joy for nearly half an hour. Though I'm not a religious person, I felt so blessed by God's grace. I feel like I am only a drop of water compared to an ocean. May the same God who put Omid in my path reward you for all the good that you do.

Omid's story is filled with miracles. As it happens, the couple who had fostered Omid were good friends of Bany's; when they had to go away for the weekend and did not want to leave Omid alone, they called Bany to ask if she and her husband would "babysit" the dog.

It was love at first sight. Bany and Bobby already had four small dogs, all rescues, at home, and even though they understood that Omid would need a tremendous amount of love and care, they couldn't resist. "We certainly weren't looking for another dog," Bany said, "but how could we walk away from this one? He needed a home!" It was, according to Bany, the best decision they ever made. "Omid has taught me so much about love and loyalty— I've never experienced such love!"

Bany Alavi-Alipour is the daughter of an Iranian diplomat and grew up in various countries around the world. Because her father was always being posted to different consulates, Bany, a devout animal lover, could never have a pet of her own. She resorted to keeping a ladybug in a little jewelry box next to her bed, a turtle in the backyard, an injured bird she had rescued in a shoebox, a lamb or a goat given to her parents as a ritual thank-you gift that was supposed to be killed for meat to feed the poor but was added to the backyard cohort instead. "My mother claimed I had turned the embassy into a zoo!" But still, she never had a dog.

"I kept begging for a dog. Then one day I came across a red, square-shaped bag in my parents' closet that had four wheels and a long shoulder strap. I placed a small pillow inside and cut one side of the shoulder strap and created … a dog with a leash! And since it had wheels, my 'dog' went everywhere with me. My parents thought it was a phase that I would grow out of; when they realized it wasn't, when we moved to America they finally gave in and agreed to get me a real dog! A black Labrador I named

Lucky. Thirty years have passed; now I *really* have a dog whom many consider very lucky and who *is* on wheels!"

Omid had—and continues to have—many angels. A man in New Jersey whose dog had recently passed away learned of Omid's story and drove to meet him and donate the wheelchair his dog had once used to Omid's new owners. Omid was able to walk for the first time in years. Later, Bany and Bobby searched online and bought Omid a new one from HandicappedPets.com.

At the annual Bark Ball, a fundraiser for the Humane Society held at the Hilton in Washington, DC, Omid was chosen Born Survivor of the year, and his photograph was featured on the cover of the summer issue of *NOVADog* magazine. More than $1 million was raised.

"Omid has brought a particular value to our life that is hard to explain," Bany says. "He has taught me a different level of love that I didn't know existed. I have had dogs for thirty-one years now and thought, *What could I possibly learn about a dog from a dog that I didn't already know?* I found out. It was the true meaning of appreciation, patience, and unconditional love.

"Sometimes I see Omid struggling, trying to maneuver after drinking water, and slipping on the wet kitchen floor. Watching him, I wonder, *Is he tired of this?* Then he notices me staring at him, and all of a sudden he gets this burst of energy and bounces to me so fast, picking up a squeaky toy as he comes to me with his happy doggie smile, that I have to laugh. I wonder at the beauty of this dog's attitude. He makes me realize life is good—be happy and enjoy the squeaky toy!

"Because who knows how long we have on this earth? When I look at Omid and all that he has gone through, I feel ashamed for some of my own weaknesses, embarrassed for the way I may have handled some situation… . I mean, look at this dog, look at this paralyzed dog, and learn from his will to survive and to be happy. How can you not be in awe of him?"

Conditions in Iran are deplorable for pets. It is not in Iranians' tradition to consider dogs as pets—except as guard dogs to be kept outside the house, where, beyond feeding, they are never given attention. To the very religious, dogs are considered unclean. The younger generation, people in their teens and early twenties, many of them animal lovers and pet owners themselves, are becoming more conscious of animal rights, rescuing dogs from the streets whenever they can. But the government, determined to crush these efforts, sends out armed patrols instructed to shoot strays on sight. People are forbidden to walk their dogs on the street; when a dog is spotted, an officer will yank its leash from the owner and take it away.

Omid's story, told worldwide, is having an effect. VAFA, the animal shelter, now has twenty-five thousand followers on Facebook. Dog lovers in Iran speak proudly of the Iranian couple from the homeland who, through Omid, have brought about a new awareness of animal rights.

Bany says, "People say to me, 'You're an angel; God bless you and your husband for saving this poor dog.' What they don't realize is, no, they don't understand. *He* saved *me*."

6

MADISON'S STORY: THE BIRTHDAY GIFT

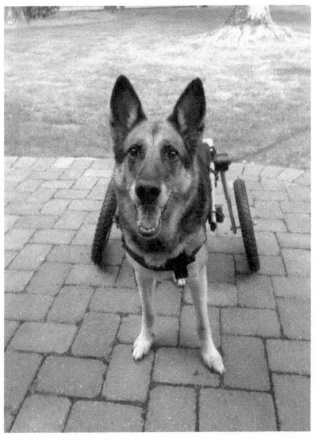

"Because of the dog's joyfulness, our own is increased. It is no small gift. It is not the least reason why we should honor as well as love the dog of our own life, and the dog down the street, and all the dogs not yet born. What would the world be like

without music or rivers or the green and tender grass? What would this world be like without dogs?"

—Mary Oliver, "Dog Songs"

On a fine, crisp September morning in 2004, Michele Pinto and her husband headed for the airport in Newark from their home in Fort Lee, New Jersey, to pick up their new puppy, shipped from a breeder in Texas. There had been some discussion about the choice of breed. Michele had grown up with dogs and was a confirmed animal lover; even so, she had always had a fear of German Shepherds. But that was her husband's absolute choice of breed, and Michele had given in to him. Once they began to pore over photographs the breeder sent, all trepidation vanished and Michele became excited. She had been longing for a dog that she could nurture and love. Now, as they waited in the cargo area at the arrivals terminal for the kennel to be brought in from the plane, Michele's excitement only grew.

The crate was brought out; they took it out to the parking lot and opened the door. Out came a chubby, four-month-old girl puppy with big, soft eyes. It was love at first sight. They named her Madison, a name Michele had always liked.

They were amazed at how easy Madison was to train. She wasn't a chewer; her only phobias were fireworks and thunder, both of which sent her running into the closet to hide. She was the perfect puppy. Michele and Madison quickly formed a bond that would take them through the difficult years that lay ahead.

Meantime, since both Michele and her husband worked, they decided Madison needed a companion. This time, Michele was eager to have another German Shepherd. They bought a male they named Baron, brought him home, and introduced him to Madison. The two became instant best friends; now there were four of them crowded into the one-bedroom, seven-hundred-square-foot apartment that was their home.

Over the next few years, Michele became increasingly aware of the cracks in her marriage, cracks that had been there for a long time but were overshadowed by the joy that Madison and Baron brought. During that time, Michele also learned that both she and her husband carried the gene for cystic fibrosis, and that childbearing was therefore risky. Her dogs were her family.

Three years later, Michele developed a set of disturbing symptoms. Extreme fatigue at first, and shortness of breath followed by inexplicable weight gain, led her to a cardiologist, who confirmed she had an acute heart condition that required immediate surgery.

That surgery proved to be what Michele describes as life awakening—a second chance to make some badly needed changes. One of those changes was a divorce. Michele saw clearly that her marriage left her feeling unappreciated and unfulfilled. Except for the deep bond she had with her dogs, her life felt empty.

But divorce had its problems: although she and her husband co-owned Baron, her beloved Madison was in her husband's name. He did not want custody of the dogs, but Michele's parents (with whom she was going to live) could not have dogs in their condo, so her husband insisted they find a foster home for Madison and Baron. Michele was devastated, so much so that she put off the divorce. Rather than give up her dogs, she would remain in an unhappy marriage for as long as she could. "The bond I had with my dogs gave me the strength—more strength than I can describe."

One day, while Michele was walking Baron, he stumbled and fell. It turned out he had fragmented bones floating in his system and needed surgery that would cost $7,000. Her husband refused to pay for it; he thought they should send the dog back to the breeder. Michele decided to go ahead with the surgery—with or without her husband's support. She held a fundraiser, baked homemade dog treats, and sold beaded jewelry pieces to raise the money. Michele explains, "At that time, Baron was the dog with all the issues; Madison was the healthy, strong, and dominant one. Madison helped me through the hard times. She was and still is my guardian angel here on Earth."

In January 2010, Michele finally filed for divorce. Fortunately, close family friends offered to take the dogs until she was able to rebuild her life.

"For the next three years, I was without my dogs. I visited them every week, provided food and vet care for them, but life without Madison and Baron was heartbreaking. It killed me."

Then Michele met Emilio and his infant son, Luca, and her life changed again. After dating for a year, they moved into a house together. "My dogs and I were together again, the bond between us as strong as ever. Luca adored the dogs, so did Emilio. Luca was like my own son. We were a family.

"That was in April. In September, I noticed that Madison acting strangely. She was constantly licking her paw, and she was dragging it so much that her nails were worn down. I made an appointment with the vet. After a series of tests, we were given the diagnosis: degenerative myelopathy, a slowly progressive, noninflammatory degeneration of the spinal cord that causes dogs to develop a nonpainful weakness of the hind legs that produces an unsteady gait. The cause is unknown, although genetic factors are suspected.

"I was devastated. I cried for three days straight. I had no idea what to expect or how much longer we would have Madison. My mission was to fight this battle with her, do whatever it took to give us more quality time together. Despite the tears, the knots in my stomach, the terrible heartache at the thought of one day having to make the dreaded decision, I was determined to get her as much time as I possibly could.

"When I learned of her illness, I whispered in her ear, 'Maddy, please give me at least until your birthday.' As I cared for her, I learned new things every day to help her get around, to eat, play, and go potty. What she taught me was strength and hope. Now I beg her, 'Please give me until Christmas.'

"I researched wheel carts for dogs," Michele recalls, "but I wasn't sure about them. It wasn't until I was speaking with our vet in early July that I heard about Walkin' Wheels. The vet told me they were easy to use, that they could help her to walk by using just her forelegs and letting the wheels help with the hind legs. And when the time came when she wasn't able to walk at all, the stirrups would provide support for her hind legs. Despite my uncertainty about how Madison might adjust to the wheels, I was determined to give it a try. We bought the Walkin' Wheels as an early birthday gift. The company, HandicappedPets.com, sent along a toy Walkin' Wheels so that Luca could understand how they were going to work.

"Putting Madison in the wheels was a great moment. The minute we strapped them onto her, she took off chasing a Frisbee! And she caught it!

"Madison has touched so many lives; all the many people who have loved her and helped us made me believe how blessed I was to have her and to understand that everything and everyone has its purpose. Ours was to help to each other.

"For Madison's ninth birthday, we had a party. Luca, who is now five, loves Madison and is always by her side, running and chasing her in her wheels. The party was really for Luca so that he may always have the memory of his favorite playmate. It may be her last birthday; I hope and pray it is not.

"My story with Madison over the past eight years has been filled with wonderful ups and terrible downs, with great sadness and boundless happiness. Most of all, it's been one of love.

"From Baron's issues to Madison's illness, I have learned the real meaning of commitment to a pet. These two dogs need me; they were meant to be my dogs, just as I was meant to be their owner. I have learned that loving as much as I do is worth every sacrifice. They are worth taking care of, they are worth rushing home for because they need to go out or eat. They are worth waking up for when they nudge you. They are worth getting up off the couch to go play with, even at eleven at night.

"The journey has been difficult, but being able to still have Madison around—to play with her, cuddle with her, smell her head, rub her ears—and just having her next to me is worth every tear I shed, every minute of sleep I lose, and whatever sacrifices I made. She has done so much for me. Her love amazes me.

"I have learned what my purpose is: it's to give all the love and compassion I have in my heart. It's to try to be better each day, even when I'm tired or not in a great mood. It's to provide a warm, loving, and happy home for Emilio, Luca, and my dogs, and to create wonderful memories for each of us. And most of all, it's being true to yourself."

7

KAYA'S STORY: A GIRL, HER DOG & THEIR WHEELS

"Perhaps one central reason for loving dogs is that they take us away from this obsession with ourselves. When our thoughts start to go in circles, and we seem unable to break away, wondering what horrible event the future holds for us, the dog opens a

window into the delight of the moment."
  — Jeffrey Moussaieff Masson

Brady believes in miracles, and in angels, too. Her life is rich with both. She looks on as her grown daughter, disabled since birth, and her dog, partially paralyzed from a spinal injury, both roll down the road at her farm in their wheelchairs. All of them are glad to be alive on this cool, blue spring day.

Mt. Hood Organic Farm is situated on two hundred acres within view of Mt. Hood, Oregon, and is home to four-and-a-half-year-old Kaya, a Pit Bull–Boxer mix, and Tonka, a huge, three-year-old Caucasian Sheepdog, plus five assorted cats. It is a working farm that produces 1.2 million pounds and twenty varieties per year of apples and pears that are packed and shipped all over the country. It is also a favored location and wedding retreat, complete with guest cottages, lakes and ponds, and farm-to-table dinners.

Last year, on the morning after Thanksgiving, Brady was shocked to find Kaya, who loves to run, lying in front of the fireplace, shaking and unable to get up. Together, she and husband, John, lifted the seventy-plus-pound dog, carried her to the car, and rushed her to the vet. After testing her feet and legs for feeling and determining that Kaya had no sensation, the vet thought she had probably suffered a severe disc injury. Quick intervention was necessary.

Brady and John were no strangers to challenges. Their eldest daughter, Ellie, now thirty-one, was born with a disability that kept her in a wheelchair. They met that challenge and managed to give Ellie a happy, loving life. Except in Kaya's case, imaging would cost $3,000. Then, if she needed surgery, that would cost another $15,000–20,000. *And* it might not work. Devastated, Brady and John looked at each other. There was no way they could come up with that kind of money. All the while Kaya was watching them, as if to say, *I'm still Kaya.*

The vet told them they must decide; it might already be too late. Kaya might never walk, might never have any movement at all. But the alternative was unthinkable, so Brady and John went home and got to work researching the problem. Is there a way to adapt, to solve feeding and potty problems, for instance? They were flying blind. Scouring the Internet, they found a site for dog wheelchairs HandicappedPets.com, that sold a fully adjustable cart called Walkin' Wheels.

They introduced the cart to Kaya gradually, watching to see what adjustments needed to be made. It *had* to work! Once the wheels were properly adjusted, Kaya, a rugged, muscular dog, took off like a downhill racer, running right alongside the huge sheepdog, Tonka. "It was as if there had never been an injury," the astonished Brady said. "And Kaya trots alongside our daughter, both in their wheelchairs, rolling down the road, happy as can be."

Brady and John enrolled Kaya in rehab two hours away in Portland, where the trainer, who is also a dog healer, announced to them after the dog began to stand on her own, "Kaya will be walking in three months!" She is on a steady trajectory to a complete recovery.

Kaya rests by doing a yoga pose, downward dog, in her wheelchair, bringing bursts of laughter from friends and guests. "She has brought such joy into so many people's lives," Brady says, choking back tears. "And to think we almost put her down."

8

JONAS'S STORY: COMPANIONS IN COURAGE

"Joyful, joyful, joyful,
as only dogs know how to be happy
with only the autonomy
of their shameless spirit."
—Pablo Neruda

Usually it's a dog that is rescued by a family; this is the story of a dog that rescued a family. When Jim and Beverly Dennis, of Deer Park, Long Island, went shopping for a pound puppy in March 2008, they had no idea that their lives were about to change forever.

The previous few years in the Dennis household had been marked by tragedy and loss. In August 2007, forty-five-year-old Jim, who worked as an operating engineer in a clean-water facility, was in a near-fatal motorcycle accident that left him with multiple fractures and nerve damage to the brain that took several months to heal. Beverly, forty-three, a former nurse, was on disability because of degenerative disc disease in her spine that continually caused her pain and numbness in her fingers and legs. Rachel, their teenage daughter living with autism, still mourned the death of her dog four years before, and their son, Mike, was in the military serving tours of duty in Iraq and Afghanistan.

As winter got ready to give way to spring, there were no signs of renewal in the Dennis household. Then one day in March 2008, Jim had the idea to surprise Rachel with a dog. He and Beverly set out on a tour of all six shelters in their area, looking for the perfect puppy. They found him at a place called Little Shelter: a four-month-old Dalmatian–Border Collie mix that had been rescued from a kill shelter in Virginia. His nose was pink, and he had a heart-shaped marking around one eye and a smile that was impossible to resist. When the volunteer lifted him out of the kennel and put him on the ground, the puppy made straight for Beverly. Beverly picked him up, nestled him in her arms, and fell in love. Jim laughed and said, "Look at that—he's a mommy's boy!"

They decided to name him Jonas (the Jonas Brothers were Rachel's favorite singing group), and the next day they took Rachel to the shelter to present her with the puppy. Rachel was speechless. She trembled with joy and burst into tears. Jim smiled; his little girl was happy.

At first Jonas was nervous. He couldn't be left alone in the house, and for the first few months, he never barked; he just stood and stared at his reflection in the blank TV screen. Jim and Beverly decided to hire a private trainer for an eight-week course. The trainer told them he suspected that Jonas had been badly abused before he was taken to the kill shelter.

For the next five years, they were a typical dog family. Jonas loved to go out in their boat, a captain's hat perched on his head; weekends he would run alongside Jim and Rachel on their 5- and 10K runs. He even enjoyed going to the spa for grooming. "Basically, he was just Jonas the family pup, who would bark at the UPS guy but lick and smooch the mailman," Beverly said.

Rachel's symptoms had lessened, her meltdowns became fewer, and she seemed more comfortable with herself, more self-confident. Jonas was the best friend she had always wanted; he was *majestic*, she said.

Since his accident, Jim had turned inward and had been self-absorbed. His injuries prevented him from doing the things he loved. Because of Jonas, he became softer and more loving toward the family. Jim claimed Beverly became calmer and emotionally stronger, more patient with everyone in the family.

When Mike came home from a tour of duty overseas, he observed the change. "This family needed that dog."

"They were wonderful years," Beverly says, a note of wistfulness creeping into her voice—because all that was about to change again. On December 3, 2012, while planning a birthday party for Jonas—his fifth—Beverly noticed he was walking with his back hunched over and was whining, as if in pain. Within three hours, he was completely paralyzed. They rushed him to the vet, who, after running tests, came up with a devastating diagnosis: intervertebral disc disease (IVDD), more common among short-legged dogs, like Dachshunds.

As a trained nurse, Beverly knew only too well what that meant: possible permanent paralysis of the hind legs, and no bowel or urine control. "We were presented with a tough decision: surgery, which may or may not work and could be dangerous, followed by months of rehabilitation and a cost that would be prohibitive for us. The other option was conventional treatment, which entailed strict, six-to-eight-week crate rest, followed by a regime of phys-

ical therapy. Since he would have no bowel or urine control, he would need round-the-clock care: changing diapers, and turning him every two hours to prevent bedsores. Jonas, at sixty-two pounds, was not a small dog.
Either way, the odds were pretty much the same. If it
turned out he was permanently disabled, there were appli-
ances, such as wheelchairs and lifting slings, that would
still enable him to have a great quality of life."

They chose the conventional treatment. Wasting no
time on grief, the three of them—Jim, Beverly, and Rachel
—swung into action. Within hours, they turned their
living room into a makeshift hospital room, stocking pain
medication, sedatives and steroids, bed pads—and diapers
by the truckload.

They made a pact: "Jonas was one of us," Beverly said,
"he was part of our family, we would not leave him alone."
They rearranged their schedules so that one of them
would always be with him, even during the night. Putting
her training to work, Beverly started passive physical
therapy to prevent atrophy, turned him every two hours to
prevent bedsores, and put him on a high-protein diet to
aid in red-blood-cell healing. The vet said Beverly was on
the right track but that she had to remember to think dog
care, not human care.

After eight weeks of complete crate rest, Jonas was able
to slide across the floor, dragging his hind legs. They
found a heavy-duty plastic laundry tub to use for hydro-
therapy and put it outside on the patio, in the sun. When
his forelegs had regained sufficient muscle, they began to
search online for some sort of wheelchair. "My husband

thought I was crazy," Beverly says, "but I remembered when I was about seven years old, we had two Papillion dogs, and one of them probably had IVDD or something similar. My dad made a homemade wheelchair for her out of training wheels from my bicycle. It worked. That was forty years ago. Let's see what they have now."

They did find dog wheelchairs on a website, HandicappedPets.com, that looked perfect, but they didn't see how they could afford one. Reading on, they learned that there was a charity, the Handicapped Pets Foundation, that was accepting applications for grants. They sent photos of Jonas and told his story: "Our dog deserves this chair."

Ten days later, on a Friday night at ten thirty, an email from the Handicapped Pets Foundation appeared in their inbox. At first they were afraid to open it. When they did, Beverly and Rachel jumped up and down and screamed, "We got the wheelchair!"

Jim wept. "We couldn't give Jonas back his legs, but he will be able to get out and walk again!"

"The moment it arrived and we hooked Jonas up to it, he looked at us with a big smile, as if to say, *I'm walking! Look at me! I'm running!*

"Now, wherever we go, people stop us and ask, 'Is that dog happy like that?' We laugh and assure them he is—*very* happy.

"Children in wheelchairs lean over to pet him; people get out of their cars to meet him and take pictures of him. They smile and give us a thumbs-up.

"Jonas has a way of sensing when a person is upset or unhappy. He'll walk right over to them and put his head on their lap."

In September, Jonas ran in the Companions in Courage race with Rachel and Jim, along with children in wheelchairs and babies in strollers. "At the corner, a woman in a wheelchair came over to us to say, 'Because of your dog, I finished this race. He inspired me.'

"At Christmastime in 2013, we took Jonas to see Santa 'Claws' at PetSmart. A gentleman came up to us with tears in his eyes and asked if he could take a picture of Jonas in his wheelchair. I said yes, of course. He then explained that his daughter is in a wheelchair and it would brighten her day to see a dog in his wheelchair. For us, that gift to that little girl was our Christmas."

Jonas, with his pink nose and heart-shaped eye, has brought the Dennis family closer together, made them—in Beverly's words—better people. Everybody, it seems, who comes in contact with him is in some way healed.

9

Hailey's Story: Wheels for Life

"I've changed my ways a little, I cannot now
Run with you in the evenings along the shore,
Except in a kind of dream, and you, if you dream a moment,
You see me there."
— Robinson Jeffers

On December 3, 1999, in the small town of Mount Barker in southern Australia, twelve-week-old West Highland White Terrier Hailey began her life as a member of the Pike household. She would be the third child to Matt and Jules and little sister to Hamish (another Westie) and Henry the Chinchilla cat, both a year older. Matt and his wife, Jules, both in their forties, had no human children.

Immediately, Hailey became the firecracker of the family. She wasn't shy about letting potential intruders know exactly where they stood and doing daily perimeter patrol, keeping guard over Hamish, Henry, and the house. Hamish was the opposite; he was the cool, calm lover. Yet they were like two peas in a pod, walking in formation, lying in formation, cuddling together. Even Henry the cat joined in the cuddle. Matt and Jules always smiled at the sight of them, a big, white, six-eyed fluffball on the couch.

For twelve years, Hailey was wonderfully happy and healthy, free of any of the typical Westie ailments, such as joint and skin issues. And twice she became a mother. Both times she had to struggle to deliver and needed the help of a veterinarian. "On reflection," Matt says, "the birthing process really put her little body through trauma; after the second litter, we decided that for her own health and well-being, we would not breed her again.

"Hailey was the greatest mother—fourteen puppies in her two litters! She was diligent about rounding them whenever they went running off in all directions. At Westie get-togethers, she was overjoyed to see all her children again."

Jules and Hailey also formed a special bond. When Jules's mother became ill with pancreatic cancer, Hailey was at Jules's side all through the illness and eventual passing. She became Jules's girl.

"It was in September of 2011, and Jules had been in Melbourne, visiting her mother. When she came home, she said, 'Did you notice Hailey scuffing her back toes as she walked?' I hadn't noticed. For the next week, we monitored her closely and saw that she was getting progressively worse. We took her to our vet, who, unable to find an explanation, took a blood test and X-ray to see if a pinched nerve might be the cause. Since basic analysis showed nothing, Hailey was given antibiotics in case it was a simple viral infection.

"As the days went by, Hailey got worse. She now had trouble controlling the back half of her spine. Alarmed, we knew we would have to find the best specialist in Australia. Luckily, two of them were in our city, Adelaide.

"Dr. Ian Douglas performed a series of tests, taking spinal- and brain-fluid samples, blood, urine, fecal samples, and numerous reflex tests. Finally, he arrived at a diagnosis: neosporosis, a parasitic disease of the spinal column that, unless caught in the very early stages, is incurable. The infection gradually leads to seizures, tremors, behavioral changes, and blindness. The eventual paralysis of the muscles involved in respiration can lead to death.

"From the time Hailey started dragging her toes, we probably knew deep down this was going to be bad. But not being able to find out what was wrong was frustrating. Not even the specialists could put their finger on it straight away. To find out later, after so much testing, that it was in fact neosporosis and therefore too late to treat with triple therapy (although we did try it) was absolutely heartbreaking. For Jules, it was a double blow: her mother was suffering from pancreatic cancer, and now her girl would be dying as well.

"For me, I had to be strong for our family, although many times I just lay on the floor alone with Hailey and cried and asked, *Why?*

"When Hailey became ill," Matt goes on to say, "she became my life. Not that she wasn't before, but now we were a team. We were not going to give in to this damn disease. We consulted the best two neurological and spinal specialists in South Australia, Dr. Ian Douglas and Dr. David Davies. The diagnosis was the same. Hailey went through test after test after test, each visit consisting of reflex testing, which she hated. Still, she struggled on. Our brave girl even sat quietly during acupuncture treatments.

"She was put on six different tablets a day, to protect her level from further deterioration, and had fortnightly checkups. As soon as I realized that Hailey would lose her ability to walk, I decided that, regardless of the outcome, she was not going to be trapped in a house for the rest of her life. I hit the Internet, searching for canine wheelchairs of all varieties on eBay, various websites, and I consulted dog forums. There was one wheelchair that I kept coming back to. It was the pink Walkin' Wheels mini. It had Hailey written all over it. It was all that I wanted for my girl—good engineering, clean lines, sophistication—and it was *pink*!

"Decision made, Hailey's wheels arrived from the other side of the world within days, and she was in them that very night. Her face blossomed, as if to say, *Thank you for giving me my freedom back.* We made videos for her Facebook followers, which warmed the hearts of many across the world with her pretty face as she trotted through the parks of Mt. Barker in the Adelaide Hills. Like the feisty warrior-princess she was, she took to her new set of Walkin' Wheels well and fully enjoyed her walks with Hamish in the park... right up until the day she could fight no longer."

Matt says his online videos showed the world "the prettiest, most courageous little Westie girl, who would not give up. We were overwhelmed by the support from around the world. Cards and gifts for Hailey arrived from the USA, Germany, and the UK. We got healing sand from holy temples, dresses and halos, handmade pendants, pretty little diaper pants....

"Being a wheelie dog provides its own challenges. One of these is getting around inside the house, or at least comfortably. We transformed our house. We covered the slippery polished-timber floors with lengths of carpet everywhere so Hailey could pull herself around by her front legs, especially when we were not able to support her rear end with a wide dressing-gown waistband. We put puppy pee pads in several places in the house, on little mattresses, which we covered in towels, making sure to hide the pee pads—to preserve a girl's dignity. We made sure Hailey always slept on the bed with one of us. We took turns, one of us on the king bed with Hailey and the other in the spare room. Hailey had half of the king bed to herself; we bordered it with neck-roll cushions covered in towels and pee pads so she wouldn't roll off the bed.

"The night of August 8, 2012, was the last night we would sleep with Hailey. On the evening of August 9, she had a bad seizure that lasted for some time. We rushed her to the emergency veterinary hospital thirty minutes away, and she was put under observation overnight. She had four more seizures during the night.

"It was at that point we had to make a decision: from here on in, it had to be about Hailey's quality of life. That would turn out to be the worst day of our life... and the end of Hailey's. Friday, August 10, 2012, at approximately 9:30 am, after a night of seizures, Hailey lost the battle and was ready for the Rainbow Bridge.

"It was the hardest thing we have ever had to do in our lives. We wrapped our arms around her on the vet's table and held her until she peacefully passed away. Then we sat with her for another hour, telling her how beautiful she was and that her fight and courage would not be in vain.

"It tears me apart still, not knowing if I did the right thing. Ending a life is not in my makeup.

"We have a photo of Hailey taken the weekend before, when we were out in the tourist town of Hahndorf, just near us, which I posted on her Facebook. I titled the photo *Angels Calling*, because it looks as if she is listening to a calling from above. Little did we know she would be called to heaven within the week."

To this day, Hailey is helping Westies in need. Matt and Jules started Hailey's Wheels for Life, a fund in her name that subsidizes a Walkin' Wheels wheelchair for dogs in need. In addition, in June 2012, Matt says, "a Facebook friend—Hamish McTavish (of the Cook family), from the UK—and I joined forces to form Hamish and Hailey's Worldwide Westie Rescue Fund. This was an important thing to do, not only to raise funds for Westies in need but also to give a purpose to Hailey's illness. Her popularity as a beautiful, pretty-faced Westie with the heart of a lion would draw much-needed funds for wonderful Westies in need throughout the world. Sir Hamish McTavish is also a popular Westie on Facebook; the two of them partnered together are a driving force in raising funds. I thank both doctors for their help and persistence; they will be made aware of Hailey's Wheels for Life, in the hope that another dog with a neurologic condition can have an extended life.

"I miss her so terribly, my courageous little pumpkin."

10

FROM THAILAND - MAMUANG'S STORY: THE MAN WHO LEARNED TO LOVE DOGS

"Dogs are the magicians of the universe."
—Clarissa Pinkola Estés, *Women Who Run with the Wolves*

When Michael Baines first moved to a small coastal town in Thailand from his home in Sweden, he was shocked by the number of homeless dogs that roamed the streets in search of food. They were known to randomly attack an unwitting person and run off into the jungle. Michael, who worked as a chef, came to fear them. They hung around in packs outside his restaurant, waiting to steal scraps of food from the garbage.

To the average Thai, a dog is just a dog, whether it's a house dog or a street dog. House dogs are allowed to run freely onto the streets and into neighbor's houses, and since they are never spayed or neutered, they invariably become pregnant and produce yet more unwanted dogs. More often than not, the unwanted puppies are abandoned, put out on the streets in a box.

For eight years, Michael ignored the street dogs or chased them away. That all changed when, one cold November night, a scrawny dog who had obviously just given birth showed up outside his restaurant, looking for food. Suddenly, Michael's heart went out to the desperate creature. He couldn't resist her pleading eyes. Every evening at five she would show up, eager and hopeful, and soon he began to take joy in giving her food and water. He named her Mamuang ("mango" in English), for the color of her coat.

One day Mamuang didn't show up. Worried, Michael waited as long as he could, until finally he had to leave and get home. The minute he arrived, he called his staff to find out if anyone had seen her. Only when he was told Mamuang had been there and been fed was he able to relax.

"That was the turning point," Michael said. "From that day on, I began to care about the other street dogs that came to the restaurant, to interact with them, and to rescue as many as I could. My wife and I began working with an organization in the area, Dog Rescue Thailand."

Soon Michael came to be known as the Man Who Rescues Dogs.

"When I first saw Coke, he was living with a family just outside the gated community where we live. A small puppy with a wagging tail and really big ears, Coke was always happy to see me and my dogs.

"One day he wasn't there. I asked the owner; she told me he had been run over by a motorbike and was lying behind the house, whimpering. The vet confirmed that the dog's back was broken and he was paralyzed. The owner asked us if we would be able to take care of him, so we decided to adopt him.

"While searching on the Internet for some sort of cart to help Coke walk, I came across Walkin' Wheels. We sent for them—they were great, very easy to use—and Coke, so fearless, so strong, took to them right away, doing amazing things like running in the woods and (almost) jumping over ditches. He actually swims with the wheels still on him! Within six months, he had worn them out.

"Then came Soda. I had taken Mamuang to the clinic for a checkup, when I saw a dog lying in a cage, apparently unable to move his back legs. I found out he was a street dog from Baan Phee, about twenty-five kilometers from where I live. Some man had beaten him with a stick, and the terrified dog had run out in the street and gotten hit by a car. He was found hiding underneath a terrace, where he'd been for two days.

"I told our vet that I would like to take Soda out of the clinic and place him in a temporary home. What I wanted to do was get him a pair of Walkin' Wheels, but because I didn't have the money myself, I had to find a way to raise the funds. Thankfully, I was able to, and after only two weeks, Soda slowly began to walk. Today he is almost running. After four weeks in his temporary home, and daily walks and visits with my gang at our home, we decided to adopt him into our family.

"I want to make Soda feel as fearless on the wheels as Coke is, and with Coke as a teacher, I think it will happen. Today, for the first time, they walked together in their wheels. It was good to see."

The man who professed to dislike and even fear street dogs now devotes a good portion of his income and much of his day—four to six hours—feeding, walking, and taking care of them. On his day off, he goes on a round to check on the dogs that Dog Rescue Thailand feeds, and at least once a week he makes a trip to the vet with a rescue, a street dog, or one of his own dogs.

Michael Baines may not be able to rescue all the abandoned and stray dogs of Thailand, but those he does stand as a symbol of how love and humanity can change not only the lives of animals but those of their rescuers as well.

11

Calypso's Story: Pretty in Pink

"I do not concern myself with my inability to feel such comfort amidst humans (other than with very few friends and family), but, rather, am simply thankful that at least dogs exist, and I'm humbly aware of how much less a person I'd be – how less a human – if they did not exist."

— Rick Bass Colter: The True Story of the Best Dog I Ever Had

Andrea and Blake Stewart, from Decatur, Alabama, were childhood friends at twelve, found each other after ten years, and married. Andrea works as a civilian environmental engineer for the US Army, and Blake works as a civilian security manager for the US Army, both on Redstone Arsenal, Alabama.

Blake already had a red six-year-old Doberman named Calypso; Andrea—or Andi, as she's called—had two cats. The first time Blake introduced Calypso to his future mommy, the sixty-five-pound pup promptly jumped onto Andi's lap and, marking Andi as her territory, peed. It was love at first sight.

Blake had chosen Caly out of her litter because she seemed the quietest and shyest. That, Blake claims, was just an act to fool him, because almost from the beginning, Caly was jumping the fence and running wild all over his (dog-friendly) neighborhood. Then Blake and Andi decided Caly needed a friend. They found an adorable little black Chihuahua–Rat Terrier–Pug mix puppy from the Decatur Animal Shelter, brought her home, and presented her to Caly. "This is your new sister," they explained, and named her Ebby, for Ebony, her shelter name. The two dogs became inseparable, playing together all day and cuddling together in their shared bed at night.

In September 2011, Andi and Blake left their home in Decatur to fly to the University of Miami (Andi's alma

mater) for a Hurricanes football game. Since they planned
to be away for ten days, they asked a friend to dog-sit.

Their trip was cut short by a phone call from their
house sitter. Calypso was "acting weird," he said. "She's
just lying still, not moving. I think you better come home."
Frantic, Andi phoned her in-laws, who lived nearby, and
asked them to take Caly to the ER. The vet, thinking it
might be a case of tick paralysis, ordered an X-ray and a
CT scan. Meanwhile, Andi and Blake scrambled to get a
flight home. Direct flights were all booked; the best they
could do was fly to Nashville. On the two-hour drive
home, they kept in constant touch with the vet.

Finally, the vet made a diagnosis. It could not have
been worse: Caly had myelomalacia, an acute, progressive
paralysis of the spinal cord that usually occurs after an
injury. Because surgery cannot stop this condition from
spreading, the narcosis of the spinal cord continues to
ascend until it paralyzes the diaphragm and ultimately
leads to death. Most dogs who receive this diagnosis must
be euthanized.

Andi and Blake put down the phone and wept the
entire rest of the drive, alternately raging and praying. By
the time they arrived at the hospital, Caly could no longer
raise her head. They called Blake's parents to ask them to
bring Ebby to say good-bye to her best friend. When Ebby
got there, Andi laid her beside Caly in the kennel.

Then the vet came in and said, "It's time."

Andi said, "We stood. I had been praying for an answer.
Now, in that moment, a voice inside me shouted, *No!* My
mind was absolutely clear; a feeling of pure, unconditional

love flooded my body and filled all my senses. '*No!*' I said aloud. 'We're not going to do this!'

"Everyone, including my husband, thought I was crazy. But I begged for more time."

Reluctantly, the vet gave in. "I'll give you twenty-four hours. But you'll regret it," he warned. "The pain will only worsen."

Andi knelt and looked deeply into Caly's eyes. "If you're willing to fight," she said, "I'm willing to fight with you."

The kennel Caly was in was huge, big enough for all three of them. Andi, Blake, and Ebby crawled inside to lie next to Caly and spent the rest of that night hugging her close.

That next morning, Caly lifted her head. To everyone's surprise, she wasn't worse.

They called one spinal expert after another, and each told them the same thing: It never ends well. If the dog does live, it will be a vegetable.

On the third day, Caly started to whine. "Do you need to go out?" Andi asked. They towel-walked her outside, and she was able to pee on her own. That she could feel the urge and use her bladder was a good sign. She was also beginning to eat the little bits of food they hand-fed her.

For five days, Andi and Blake kept a vigil; one of them was always at her side. The techs, who by then had bonded with Caly, set up a room—exam room 3—for Andi and Blake where they could work on their laptops or watch movies. "We *lived* in that room—we even slept there," Blake says. The four of them became favorites with the staff. One of the techs, who lived an hour away, even came in on his day off to hand-feed Caly.

When finally they were able to take Caly home, one of the first things Andi and Blake had to figure out was a way to get her outside to go potty. Blake was able to carry her, but Andi had to use a harness. Then, "Picture this," Andi explains: "Either Blake or I stand over Caly, bracing her with our knees. Her butt is facing the same way we are looking, and her head is just under our butt. This is how we have to get into the squatting position to go potty. Now imagine seeing this as you drive down our street. Not sure what people thought. One morning around four, the cops drove by and actually lit Blake up with a spotlight! I promised them we weren't hurting our dog—just helping her pee.

"When workmen from Decatur Utilities came to cut down a tree in our yard, one of them stared at me standing on the lawn, trying to relieve Calypso's bladder. There I was, straddling Calypso's shoulders with my knees and cradling her hips in my arms. She was peeing and barking at him at the same time. He didn't ask what I was doing to my dog, but he did look a little frightened. Who knows what ungodly thing he thought I was doing!

"The day before we left the vet hospital with Caly, we began to research various solutions for living with a handicapped pet and found a website, HandicappedPets.com. The vets advised against our buying a wheelchair right away. I guess they thought we might not be able to manage, and, since they were sure we would be bringing her back to euthanize her, they wanted to save us some money. But I listen about as well as Caly does and I am just as headstrong, so I ordered the chair on Friday and had it overnighted to arrive on Saturday morning. The shipping charges were more than the chair!"

Once they got the wheels on Calypso, it took about six seconds before the dog was off and running, causing a traffic jam in the neighborhood. A huge dog running down the street in a pink wheelchair was a sight to behold.

Then Andi and Blake heard about a holistic vet in Nashville, Dr. Berschneider, who used acupuncture, chiropractic, and various other alternative treatments, and decided to give her a try. Within weeks, Caly was beginning to regain movement in her hind legs.

Andi posted this message on their Facebook page:

Tonight while we were in Nashville at Calypso's acupuncture/chiropractor appointment, we met a lady in the lobby who was crying because she had just found out her dog had bulging discs and was possibly facing paralysis. They were in the middle of trying to find someone/anyone in a one-hundred-mile radius to perform surgery on her dog. I walked right up to her and hugged her, gave her my cell phone number, and told her that I knew exactly what she was going through, that this exact moment was excruciatingly hard and not many people could or would understand that, but that I did and that I also knew things would get better. Calypso was an "absolute worst-case scenario," and look at us now—we're surviving and thriving. I [told this woman] if she ever needed anything, even in the middle of the night, anything at all, just please call me, even though she didn't even know me. I promise you that I have never been hugged back so hard in my life. And as it turns out, she ended [up] being referred from Nashville to Decatur to Dr. Michael Newman, one of Calypso's vets. I reassured her that she was in good hands with him and reiterated that she could call anytime. Tonight my prayers are with this woman ... and for anyone else who is struggling. I know. I've been there. I have your back with all the prayers I can pray and all the love I can give. It's the least I can do, because this is what was shown to me. Pay it forward, my friends, and God bless!!!

Andi says, "It's been almost two years to the day since we came home early from vacation to our sweet Calypso, who had suddenly become paralyzed. It was a no-brainer for me, her mommy, to save her, but it's been a long, hard road. We've spent a small fortune, and we've even lost friends (some people can be cruel when you're down), but no matter—we know that we made the right decision, and we are grateful every day for that opportunity. However, one thing that strikes me as funny is that no matter how amazing Calypso proves to be (running and even *jumping* in her wheels), it never fails to surprise me that people will come up to us and say, 'Oh, how sad. Oh, she's pitiful. That's heartbreaking. Bless her heart.'

"No. It's *not* sad. It's *not* pitiful. It's *not* heartbreaking. But yes, you can still bless her heart. Randomly, Caly was dealt a bad genetic hand. She's paralyzed. We know. So what? She's *amazing*. We're not sad and pitiful and crying and depressed—and trust me, neither is she. We could all learn a lot from Calypso. She's happy and fun and full of energy and life. Tell me how that's sad and pitiful. You wouldn't say that to a human in a wheelchair. Please quit saying that about my dog or any other dog in carts. Praise her instead, and celebrate her for being a fighter, for being strong, and for showing her family, her friends, and an entire community that love conquers all!"

12

DEXTER: THE WOUNDED WARRIOR

Dex and his owner Curtiss Lindsay upon receiving Dex's Started Hunting Retriever title in West Mississippi.

"Percy does not like it when I read a book.
He puts his face over the top of it, and moans ....
But Percy, I say, Ideas! The elegance of language! ....
Books? says Percy. I ate one once, and it was enough. Let's go."
  —Mary Oliver, *Red Bird*

Puppy love—real puppy love—never grows old. The absolute, unconditional love in a dog's eyes as he gazes up at us teaches us a little more about how to be human, and for those graced with the heavy responsibility of being a caregiver to pets with chronic illness or disability, it inspires a deeper sense of compassion.

This is the story of what former staff sergeant Curtiss Lindsay learned from Dexter, his four-year-old Labrador Retriever, who has been in a wheelchair from the time he was a three-month-old puppy. He is a warrior, too—and a champion.

Curtiss teaches eighth-grade math at the Louisiana School for Agricultural Science; his wife, Sherlyn, is a pharmacist at the local long care facility. They are both lifelong dog lovers.

In September 2006, ten months after Staff Sergeant Curtiss Lindsay returned to his home in Louisiana from an eighteen-month tour of duty in Iraq, Sherlyn presented him with a four-month-old Chocolate Labrador Retriever for his birthday. They named her Paige. For Curtiss, who had grown up hunting and fishing, Paige turned out to be the best hunting dog he'd ever had—or seen, for that matter.

On a cold day in February 2009, Paige went into the whelping box Curtiss had set up for her in a heated room separate from the house and gave birth to nine puppies, seven males and two females, all seemingly healthy. The last of the litter, the runt, was a male. After about a week, Curtiss and Sherlyn noticed that the little one was not moving his back legs. Alarmed, they took him to their veterinarian. The vet took a set of X-rays, but since the puppy's bones weren't sufficiently formed to show any damage, he assumed that it was a severe inflammation that had caused temporary paralysis and prescribed dexamethasone to reduce the swelling. However, when it became clear that the paralysis was permanent, not temporary, he held out no hope; the pup should be put down. If Curtiss continued to refuse euthanasia, the vet told him not to bring the dog back.

Curtiss could not, would not, think of it. He had seen too much on the battlefields of Iraq not to appreciate the preciousness of life—all life. He decided he would give the pup every chance in the world to make it. He told the vet they were taking the little guy home.

They took to calling him Dex (short for the medication he was on—the name stuck) and tried their best to take care of him at home. But several weeks later, little Dex suddenly became very ill. They took him to another veterinarian, forty-five miles away, who had more sophisticated equipment. That vet, Dr. Melanie Toal, came up with a completely different diagnosis: Dex had not been *born* paralyzed, she said; right after birth, his mother had apparently accidentally stepped on the tiny pup, dislocating his rear hips and breaking both his hind legs.

Initially, Dr. Toal had her professional reservations about trying to help Dex. He was so frail, and his future too uncertain. As the Lindsays pleaded their case to her, Sherlyn had the idea of showing her a YouTube video they had posted of Dex in a homemade cart, retrieving a stuffed animal. They had constructed a crude wheelchair out of a piece of wood, a couple of casters, and some bungee cord. This new device enabled Dex to retrieve, and he loved the speed it gave him.

After viewing the video, Dr. Toal agreed to help, under three conditions: Dex had to have a good quality of life, he had to have appropriate indoor living space for his condition, and the animal hospital would not release him until he had some type of transportation to support the normal, active lifestyle of a Labrador Retriever. Dr. Toal could see what a happy puppy Dex was, wagging his tail and giving kisses, and she wanted to support their decision, but she also had to explain to them how serious his injuries were. His fractures had cut off the flow of blood to his legs, causing the skin to break down and become infected. Dex would have to begin a course of antibiotics, and, worse, both of his hind legs would have to be amputated.

In Iraq, Curtiss had witnessed many battlefield injuries that had led to amputation, and he had watched a buddy die from loss of blood. "Some nights I would sit with Sherlyn, worrying and wondering if we were doing the right thing. When one of us would get down, the other would step in with words of encouragement. Finally, we came to the decision that if ever Dex seemed in pain—if his tail stopped wagging and he was clearly not happy—that would let us know he'd had enough. But as long as he kept giving us kisses and asking for ear scratches and wagging his tail, we would get through it with him.

"Dex pulled through both amputations beautifully. But the question remained, what does one do with a two-legged Labrador Retriever? The amputations were too high up on the legs to fit him with prosthetics, and Labs are active dogs. To limit his mobility to two legs was definitely cause for concern.

"Perhaps this is where I should talk about Dex's fighting spirit and his larger-than- life drive. He doesn't realize that he is different; he still has the playful nature of any Lab puppy. At three months, he was already retrieving our Maltese's little bunny rabbit, dragging his two useless legs behind him. He is by far the happiest dog I've ever met. Even during the months of pain and hardship he had to endure, he never had a single day of depression. He is truly an inspiration.

"After much research, we located Walkin' Wheels. We purchased a wheelchair, and it changed all of our lives forever. In giving him the gift of mobility, this chair has given Dex his life back. He loves to go on long walks with us, and he keeps up with other dogs just fine, even chasing his Maltese sister around the island in the kitchen! And he loves to swim. He is a messy swimmer, but a swimmer nonetheless. We removed the wheels and put him in a floater, but one day the floater came off and he just kept right on swimming without it.

Dex the two-legged Lab also promises to be the great duck hunter his mother, Paige, was. He was accepted into his local Hunting Retriever Club, and at the tender age of just one year, he earned his HRC Started title at the hunt test, a four-day event divided into two types of evaluations: a land series and a water series. In each, dogs are evaluated for their natural retrieving desire, memory, marking ability, and obedience to their handler's commands. The tests try to simulate actual hunting situations at realistic hunting ranges, with the handlers wearing appropriate hunting attire and firing a shotgun loaded with blanks.

Dex has also met handicapped veterans through the Tower of Hope Foundation, an organization that helps to train service dogs for injured veterans. Dex would roll up in his wheelchair, his tail wagging vigorously, next to a veteran in a wheelchair. The surprised veteran would give him a huge smile and say, "Hey, buddy! Wanna race?"

Dex has also become part of Curtiss's teaching strategies and is allowed on occasion to attend Curtiss's classes. The students know and love him, and his presence has taught them lessons not found in textbooks: that love is unconditional, and that physical capabilities do not have to be obstacles but are merely opportunities to become more creative. Dex has also been a wonderful companion for students who struggle with reading. It is not unusual to find a student sitting on top of Dex's dog bed in the corner of the classroom, reading quietly to him, Dex's head resting in the student's lap.

"In January 2014, through much hard work, determination, and perseverance, Dex earned the title of Started Hunting Retriever at the hunt test in Vicksburg, Mississippi. The first watermark of the weekend was by far the longest swim of his life, but Dex would not back down from it. He belly-flopped into the water and swam his little heart out until he reached the mark; then he turned around and swam back. When his tired body left the water to return the bird to hand, his tail was still wagging.

"When Dex was going through his surgeries for the double amputation, we did not know what sort of life he was going to be able to lead. But he has never slowed down, never given up, never taken no for an answer, and never accepted anything as an obstacle. He has taught us a great deal more than we could ever teach him. Dex has taught us never to give up. He knows no limitations. He adjusts to whatever life throws at him. I hope people will think about him the next time they have a bad day."

Curtiss still has episodes of PTSD. An unexpected shot or fireworks or a war movie might set him off; when it does, Dex pushes against him and takes Curtiss's hand very gently in his mouth to remind him his dog is near.

"Dex has been medicine for my soul. As my best friend and confidant, he knows things about me that no one else knows. He is always by my side when I'm home and worries when I leave him, even for a few seconds. Throughout his life, he has always wanted to please us as much we want to please him. Just today, we were sitting on the back porch with him lying beside us, each of us enjoying our time together."

These two warriors have much to be grateful for, not the least of which is the extraordinary love and loyalty they share.

13

FROM CHINA, WANG WANG'S STORY: ADOPT AND CHERISH

Xiaoli, WangWang, and Mark C. Robinson

"If you don't own a dog, at least one, there is not necessarily anything wrong with you, but there may be something wrong with your life."

– Roger A. Caras

WangWang's story is both sad and heroic, very much like China itself. Her story is set in the beautiful, rich county of Ledong, in Hainan. Sometimes called a "green treasure house" and "a land of cashew nuts," Ledong has a beautiful natural landscape and an ancient seascape that make it a popular tourist destination.

But there is a dark side to this otherwise culturally developed county: the slaughter of dogs for food, a practice that has long been hugely offensive to many in China. A not-uncommon sight on the streets is a dog-smuggling truck crammed with dogs on their way to slaughter. The drivers stop to capture any dog on the street and throw it into one of the cages in the back of the truck. If the dog should struggle to get away, the driver will shoot it—all in plain sight of young children and their dogs. Animal activists continually call for an end to this inhumanity, as well as for an end to the practice of eating dogs.

Historically, Chinese emperors were the only people allowed to own dogs. The favorite was the small, lion-like Pekingese; the Empress Dowager Cixi of the Qing dynasty, the last imperial dynasty, was said to have owned over a hundred of them. But in 1966, during the Cultural Revolution, the public rebelled against the wealthy bourgeois whose dogs were better fed than much of the population and were considered a symbol of abundance and waste. What followed was the slaughter of dogs by the tens of thousands.

In the 1990s, Deng Xiaoping, often credited with advancing China toward a free-market economy, owned two dogs. It is possible that his influence paved the way to the eventual acceptance of dogs as pets today. Nevertheless, the killing goes on.

Lucy Wang, animal-rights activist with the World Grassroots Alliance for Paws in China, feels she must add —not in defense, but as an explanation—"Let me state for the record that, in my opinion, the people themselves are not to blame. Neither is Chinese traditional culture. People have become indifferent or insensitive, perhaps because they have been indoctrinated to be so, particularly under Mao, when sympathy for the downtrodden, love of pets, wearing makeup, and displaying individual taste in fashion were all condemned as bourgeois and rebellious."

In October 2012, a skinny, dirty dog dragged itself into the yard of a construction site, littered with trash and dead leaves and patches of dry, brittle stalks of grass, to lie exhausted amid discarded bags of cement. Xiaoli (pronounced Shou-Lee), a woman well known for her love of animals, received a call from her coworkers to tell her about the dog and rushed out to the yard.

What she saw tore her heart apart. An adorable small female dog with large, expressive eyes and a baby-doll turned-up nose was dragging herself along the ground in search of food and water, with only her front legs for support. The rear portion of her little body seemed to be paralyzed, and areas on both of her back legs were badly injured from being dragged along the hard ground. Even though the dog was barely alive, she was starved for attention and begging to be petted.

Xiaoli quickly found a safe place for her in the back room of the site's cafeteria and rounded up some eggs. "The poor thing practically inhaled six eggs and drank a huge bowl of water." Xiaoli could not imagine what this dog had suffered and how she had made it this far. For a week, she took care of the dog at the construction site and set up a fundraiser for her care. She named her Wang-Wang, which in English means "hope."

When Xiaoli took her to the animal hospital, X-rays showed WangWang's thoracic spine had been fractured so badly that it had shattered into many pieces. The vet believed WangWang had been severely beaten with a heavy object. Horrified, Xiaoli wondered what kind of sick, heartless person could so savagely hurt a fragile and defenseless dog.

Days later, she learned who that person was: an elderly man who happened to be an employee of the very same construction company where Xiaoli worked. Apparently, the man had spotted the dog playing in an area near the construction site where he planted his vegetables. Furious that the animal had damaged some of his plants, he hit her with such force that he broke her spine. A witness said the man then just stood and watched as the injured dog, unable to run, dragged herself away from him in fear.

WangWang's story drew immediate attention. Compassionate and caring people from miles around responded, and an online campaign began. Xiaoli was able to raise over US$600 for WangWang's medical treatment.

There are no animal-cruelty laws in place in China; Xiaoli was therefore not able to press charges against the man who had hurt WangWang. But his brutal act so outraged animal lovers that an online mob formed and demanded to know the man's identity and contact information so that they could publicly condemn him and threaten retaliation. Xiaoli, however, decided not to take any aggressive actions against the man. She vowed instead to devote her time and energy to giving WangWang the best quality of life and all the love she had in her heart.

With the help of donations, Xiaoli was able to get WangWang's injuries treated. She underwent surgery in which a titanium rod was placed in her spine to stabilize the fractures; still, WangWang would be permanently paralyzed, never again able to use the back half of her body.

Lucy Wang explains, "Together Animal Aid Center is our associated rescue center in Beijing-China. Our volunteer Xiaoli, who rescued WangWang, came to me and told me about WangWang's condition and the difficulties she was having finding a decent wheelchair for [the dog] in China, and inquired about the possibility of getting one from America.

"We immediately started the search for the right wheelchair for WangWang, contacting several companies that manufacture them. We also inquired about the possibility of getting a discount, considering the limited funds the shelter has. A company in America, Walkin' Wheels, replied and offered to donate a new wheelchair to Wang-Wang.

"After researching the company, the product, and customer feedback, I found that the Walkin' Wheels cart not only is well designed but also was manufactured by a company with the highest moral and professional ethics."

In spite of the terrible misfortune and injustice of WangWang's injuries, she is now living a life with love and comfort in Xiaoli's shelter with other rescued animals.

Given China's current undeveloped animal rights and welfare, WangWang in her new wheelchair is both a story of rehabilitation and a powerful message to Chinese society about how animals should be treated and valued.

Fortunately, things are changing for the better. Today, China has an estimated 130 million dogs, many of whom are household pets. As a result, the country's animal-protection community is expanding.

WangWang's story has touched the hearts and opened the minds of many. A new sign over the dog-rescue shelter door reads Adopt and Cherish.

About The Author

Sandy Johnson, a former actress, is the author of 7 previously published fiction and nonfiction books. She has traveled to more than 40 countries meeting and interviewing spiritual leaders, shamans and healers, including His Holiness the Dalai Lama, who wrote the forward to her *The Tibetan Book of Elders*. Published in several languages, her books have been listed on the *New York Times Best Books of the Year*, been a Literary Guild selection, and been featured in *People*, as well as other major publications. Her most recent novel, *The Black Pope*, was inspired by the powerful healers and shamans she had encountered during her extended visits to Brazil.

Miracle Dogs: Adventures on Wheels is the first of a series of her current non-fiction project.

Johnson lives in Los Angeles where she also teaches classes in journal writing, *Write Yourself Well*.

BOOKS BY SANDY JOHNSON

The Cuppi
Walk a Winter Beach
Against the Law
The Book of Elders
The Book of Tibetan Elders
The Brazilian Healer with the Kitchen Knife
Mystics and Healers
The Thirteenth Moon; a Journey into the Heart of Healing
The Black Pope (coming soon)

See http://www.SandyJohnsonAuthor.com

Appendix 1: Mystics and Healers by Sandy Johnson

INTRODUCTION

My travels into the world of mystics and healers began in 1991, when I ceased being an author, mother, teacher, divorcee, hiker, skier, pilot, dog lover-and became a statistic: the one woman in eight diagnosed with breast cancer each year over her lifetime, according to the Journal of American Medicine.

I chose the conventional medical route not out of conviction, but out of fear. I knew there were less invasive, less draconian alternatives, and I gave them a hard look. But to choose those roads took courage and unshakable faith, and at the time I did not possess enough of either.

And so, in crisis mode, every nerve in my body on high alert, I entered the world of white-coated wizards with their triple threat treatment: surgery (I opted for a lumpectomy), chemo, and radiation.

In crisis mode there is no place for tears. But then two weeks into chemotherapy on one rare summer day when the mountains were streaked with fiery copper, the sky a shimmering turquoise, I decided to drive out into the desert. With not another car in sight, I could speed along, windows open, and feel the sweet juniper-scented air on my face.

Suddenly I had the strangest sensation. I could feel a whole clump of my hair being ripped from my head. I looked at my side-view mirror and saw it drifting down the road like tumbleweed, stopping when it clung to a cedar tree. r felt another piece of hair fly off. I screeched to a halt at the side of the road, rolled up all the windows, leaned against the steering wheel, and sobbed.

A year-and-a-half later, rounds of treatment completed, the doctor pronounced me cancer-free. Chances of a recurrence would begin to decrease after five years, the doctor explained, and reeled off a timetable of percentages, which I could not hear. Recurrence? Five years? Percentages? I don't call that cancer free; I call that cancer maybe-if-it doesn't-come-back free.

Fatigued and weak, my head covered with the soft, downy fuzz of a baby chick, my face naked without eyebrows, I felt like a survivor of a bombed-out city, stumbling around in the rubble of my body.

I knew I needed to get strong, and to improve my immune system so that five or seven years down the road it wouldn't strike again. New Agers, with their theories of why it had happened and what lessons cancer had to teach me made me break out in hives. Yet at the same time I think I knew that as long as there were still demons lurking in the dark corners of my soul real healing might not be possible. Mind, body, and spirit are one. The white-coated wizards had done what they knew how to do to treat-or even cure the disease. But the soul healing would have to come from me.

My sons who had been flying back and forth to be by my side had gone back to their lives; I had a book to finish, one which entailed crisscrossing the country to interview and record the wisdom of the American Indian-much of it by car on unpaved and unmarked reservation roads.

Death had nodded in my direction; I nodded back and moved on. At dawn one morning I got up, packed my tape recorder and notebook, tied a scarf around my awful wig, and took off.

Medicine men and women in various tribes I visited, when they learned I had just been through a life-threatening illness, offered me their own medicines to counteract the effects of chemo and radiation: healing herbs, root extracts used for hundreds of years. And ceremonies. Sweat Lodges in the Plains, all-night Medicine Sings with the Hopi. In the Northeast, I learned to draw a Medicine Wheel. In Colorado, I took peyote that turned my insides out.

Over the next year my hair grew back (a different color), strength returned: perhaps due to the Native medicines, or maybe modern Western science had done its job. In any case, the white-coated wizards were impressed with my lab results. You're fine, they said, go forth and multiply (books, that is).

Soon after the publication of my book on Native American elders, my publisher asked me to write a similar book about Tibetans. Since the Chinese communist invasion in 1950 and subsequent occupation, Tibetans have been living in exile, mostly in India. Dharamsala, in the north, is the seat of the government-in-exile and the current home of the Dalai Lama. I had written His Holiness earlier to request a meeting to discuss my project and gave the dates I expected to be in India. Before the appointed day of my interview, I spent a month getting acquainted with the people of Shangri-La, or in Tibetan, Shambala, the Hidden Kingdom, whose teachings had remained secret for thousands of years.

The similarities between Native Americans and Tibetans were striking. Tibetan oracle-priests and Native American shamans both practice dream-travel, similar ceremonies, meditation, and telepathy. Both cultures also believe in karma, religion as a way of life, and believe that time is circular, non-linear.

My first encounter with mystical healing was with a seventy-five year-old Tibetan nun who had recently escaped the Chinese when they attacked her abbey in Tibet. She lived in a tiny dwelling down the hill from the Dalai Lama's residence. I met her the day before my scheduled appointment with His Holiness and remember remarking on her apparent good health after such an ordeal. Shaved head, and not a tooth in her mouth, there

was something beautiful about her, a radiance, a gleeful-
ness.

Through the translator, she said, "Only a week ago I
was blind and couldn't walk." Then she told her story:
"We crossed the mountain on foot through snow and ice
under cover of dark, just like His Holiness had in 1959. It
wasn't until we crossed the border into India that we were
taken in and fed and given horses. My whole family had
been killed by the Chinese, and many nuns at the abbey
had been arrested and tortured, but I had to get to Dharamsala to see the Dalai Lama before I died. For my family.
For the other nuns. It was my one wish.

"But when I got here, I was too sick. I couldn't walk, my
eyes had gone blind from the snow. And so I just sat here
in this little room and meditated. Months went by-I don't
know how long-people brought me tea and tsampa (dried
barley]-then one day a week ago, two men appeared at my
door. They said they had come to take me to see His Holiness. They picked me up and carried me to a car and drove
me up the hill to the residence.

"His Holiness welcomed me and called me Ani Gom-
chen, which means Great Meditator. He stroked my head
and recited mantras, and then blew three times on the top
of my head.

"All of a sudden I could see! I could look right into his
face. And I got up-I stood straight up and walked!"
Smiling, her eyes brimming with tears of joy, she stood
and took a few long strides to demonstrate. "I walked all
the way down the hill to my house.

I remember thinking at the time that the nun's sponta-
neous healing had been triggered by a state of ecstasy, not
unlike the people who throw away their crutches after
being tapped on the head by a TV evangelist. But then the
next day, I met with the Dalai Lama. As I sat talking to him
and felt the full force of his joy, compassion, and all-
encompassing love, I wasn't so sure. And when I got back
to my hotel, I noticed the "Delhi-belly" that had felled me
the night before, that had me doubled over even into the
morning wondering how I would keep my appointment
with the Dalai Lama, had completely disappeared. Had
my excitement and anticipation of the meeting created an
ecstatic state similar to that of the nun's? Or was it in fact
the Dalai Lama's famous loving kindness and compassion
that caused my healing?

It seemed my nodding acquaintance with cancer and
mortality had set me on a path that would take me
through a strange and mysterious maze of smoke and mir-
rors and bottles of snake oil, and at times send me tum-
bling down the rabbit hole.

Medical miracles or imagined healings born of an
intense desire to believe? Hard to say, but I packed up my
laptop, my tape recorder, and my notebook and once
again took to the road, this time the road leading to mystics and healers from around the world, determined to
solve the mystery.

I've witnessed psychic surgery in Brazil to remove a
cancerous rumor without anesthesia from a man's
stomach, sleight-of-hand surgery in the Philippines during
which the "healer" palmed a piece of chicken liver pur-

chased at the corner stall, and a simple housewife in Florida who goes into a trance and manifests flakes of gold on her skin and, with a second-grade education, quotes medieval French verses. I've also met a housewife-turned-healer in Idaho who commands healings from God.

During my exploration I would experience my own mysterious disappearance of the flu during a healing done over the phone. I would be taken on a shamanic journey to a forest in the "lower world" and to a cloud in the "upper world" and to an event buried deep in my past to meet one of my demons.

And hands so skillful, so intuitive they can only have come directly from the gods. I don't mean laying-on of hands, either, I mean finding the exact location in the body where fear lives. Or grief. Or anger, or loss. The place where toxic tears are stored: fertile ground for illness to take root. And then throwing open the windows of all those dark places and flooding them with air and sunlight.

Celebrity healers who had turned their gift into a multimedia business were of little interest to me, due perhaps to my exposure to the teachings of Native American shamans. They believe that to profit from the gift given by the Great Spirit is to have it taken away or worse, suffer personal punishment. Small donations as tokens of gratitude seemed reasonable, but one healer I came across had people sign a contract promising to pay tens of thousands of dollars in advance.

I also ran across the charlatans (look for the diamond-encrusted Rolex and the Rolls and the misty-eyed groupies often called "students"); and the deluded ones, those who truly believe they are healers, and who with their good intentions and loving natures often do bring about some sort of a healing—generally not lasting.

But then, seemingly out of nowhere and when least expected, there is the rare gem: the humble and unfailingly honest miracle maker.

Buy this book from Amazon.com [http://www.amazon.com/Mystics-Healers-Travels-Shamans-Miracle-Makers/dp/1419689312/ref=pd_sim_b_3]

Appendix 2: The Thirteenth Moon by Sandy Johnson

THE THIRTEENTH MOON
A Sea Change in the Land of Cancer
by Sandy Johnson

JANUARY - MOON OF THE TERRIBLE

Amid the cold and deep snows
of midwinter, the wolf packs
howled hungrily outside Indian
villages. The people kept the
fires going and sang their
songs until they could no
longer hear the sound of
the wolves.

(Sioux)

On a table in the living room is a collection of carved turtles that I picked up during my travels through Indian country for *The Book of Elders: Life Stories & Wisdom of Great American Indians,* miniatures fashioned from stone, bronze, pewter and other materials. I pick up a silver one that I bought at a trading post near the Pine Ridge Indian Reservation in South Dakota and turn it over in my hand, remembering. The owner of the store had explained that the turtle represents Earth.

"See, there are 13 large scales on Old Turtle's back, one for each month of the year," he said.

When I looked at him quizzically, he explained, "*Lakota moons did not follow today's twelve-month calendar; the Lakota moons followed each season. Spring, summer and fall each had three moons, while winter had four.*"

He pointed to the small scales that surround the large ones. "These 28 small scales represent each day in a lunar month. All together, they hold the key to the mysteries of the moon." Then he added, "For those who know how to look."

The way the ancients kept track of the seasons was to give names to each of the full moons.

As the months unfolded during my year of living tremulously, there were moons that watched as I walked purposefully, head erect, spine straight, but there were also times when the moon's face—the goddess whose light ruled the night—was turned away from me. Those nights were silent and dark, and I staggered and stumbled. Once or twice, when no one was around to see, I even melted into a puddle of grief. But still no tears. Never tears.

In this Moon of the Terrible, I am in the land of hospital waiting rooms. I am assigned a patient number and a new ID by an admittance person with alarmingly long blood-red nails. She somehow manages to type my entire medical history, along with a good deal of my personal story, into a computer. Marriages, divorces, pregnancies, children, smoking, drinking, drugs. Do I wear a seat belt while driving? *What???* Then come the doctors, the ones the Hopi call the White Coats. The oncologist looks distressed and mumbles something in my general direction.

"Sorry?" I ask. He simply mumbles louder in reply. I get the words "incurable...controllable..." but I don't get which one applies to me.

On the other hand, my own doctor hugs me and, misty-eyed, assures me that I can beat this. He even tells me how: with my mind. Keith Agre is not a power-of-positive-thinking kind of guy. He's a pragmatist who understands me and how fiercely determined I am. He explains it all carefully and in terms I can understand. Although Keith would be quick to deny it (with a groan and a roll of his eyes), he is a healer. His compassion is real, and so is his optimism, which is contagious.

Billy is at my side taking notes. I have the feeling he is also keeping an eye on me to make sure I don't bolt for the door and run off to one of my shamans to drink potions made from the eyeballs of boiled rattlesnakes. Or to Brazil to one of the healers I wrote about. Which is what part of me wants to do. The part of me that longs for magic.

Somehow I don't, though. It's out of my hands now. I have entered the Land of Cancer, governed by White Coats, through a passageway where I am blindfolded, spun round and round, and pointed in one direction or another. If there is a door leading out, I cannot see it.

Billy and I share many of the same sensibilities, with the exception of anything remotely related to the world of healers, the very mention of which will drive him right out of his linear, strong-minded and quite opinionated head. When my book on healers came out a couple of years before, he made no bones about hating the subject matter (though he was careful to preface his remarks by saying he thought the book was well written).

This middle son of mine, with his father's darkly serious eyes, has grown to be my protector. Not just because he is the one who lives in L.A., but because it has always been his role in the family. I'm guessing he feels what I need protecting from is myself.

January 20, 2006

Hi Everyone,

I apologize for the mass e mail. I've spoken to all of you at least once since the original report on Jan. 13, and now that more info is in I thought it easiest to just get everyone on the same page.

Here's the update: After weeks of waiting, punctuated by a variety of tests and scans, we've arrived at a diagnosis of Sandy's cancer and have been given a suggested course of treatment.

Basically, she's got a high-grade cancer which has metastasized to other areas of her body from the original site in her kidney. This type of cancer (a relatively uncommon form of kidney cancer) has no known cure, and the goal is to control it through chemotherapy. The treatments are not expected to bring on hair loss or extreme nausea.

The plan to remove her kidney was abandoned when the metastases were discovered; the diseased kidney is still functioning well and will be needed to remove the

byproducts of the chemotherapy. Also she'll be stronger if she hasn't just had an organ removed.

The pain is being controlled to some extent by vicodin, which makes her a bit loopy at times, so she uses it judiciously. Sitting upright for extended periods causes her a lot of discomfort (it's kind of like a bad case of sciatica), so don't invite her to a Wagner opera or a long dinner until the pain begins to subside, hopefully soon.

She looks great, by the way, and she is her usual loving wonderful self through all of this.

Though she feels a little overwhelmed right now, my sense is that your calls and even visits/invitations will be most welcome in the coming days and weeks.

We are going to be actively seeking other opinions before the proposed chemo starts on Thursday. If your first cousin just got the Nobel for nephro-oncology, now's the time to pick up the phone. On the other hand, if you have a healer in Sedona you want her to meet, please be reminded: she wrote the book — literally — on faith/alternative healers, and as of this time she has chosen not to contact any of the many interesting individuals depicted therein.

Thank you for all of your calls and support.
Billy

They fly in: Mark, the eldest, from New Hampshire; Anthony, the youngest, from New Mexico; Sally from Florida; Wendy from Northern California. Debbie, who lives in New York with her two boys, is in the middle of a nasty divorce; she writes thoughtful, loving notes. We are a tight tribe, we Johnsons—do not mess with us. We close ranks and guard each other fiercely. Their love takes my breath away.

Sally is in town to give an acting workshop with Dee Wallace. She has set aside extra days to go with me to medical appointments. Sunday, Billy and his wife HJ make us one of their elaborate brunches of poached eggs, bacon (Why not?), English muffins, fresh fruit and steaming cappuccinos.

Billy and Sally are laughing, swapping stories about their father's sometimes riotously quirky behavior (getting on an airplane in his sheepskin bedroom slippers... how he used to reach over and grab the steering wheel—his way of giving directions). HJ and I are discussing the pros and cons of having two kids practically in one litter (their boys are 14 months apart) or having them as I did, five years apart.

Afterward, Sally and I go outside and sit on the hammock, little boys crawling all over us. When they run off,

Sally puts her head on my shoulder and cries. I feel such love for them; they are my reason.

Moments like these makes me think this moon doesn't seem all that terrible. Until toward the end of it, on the 27th day. I am in Keith Agre's office for a routine appointment. I am sitting on the examining table talking to Billy, who sits in the chair facing me as Keith, standing behind me, makes his examination: listening to my heart, tapping my back to check the lungs. Then he feels around my neck, stopping when he comes to the area of my right collarbone.

"What's this?" he asks.

I put my hand there. I don't feel anything. Maybe a tiny bump.

"I think we need to have this biopsied," he says.

I look across at Billy, then I turn to Keith and frown disapprovingly, as though he has just stepped out of line. I had agreed to something bad in my kidney, but that's all I signed on for. Do not go poking around looking for more trouble.

I probably didn't say any of this.

On the way home, Keith calls me on the cell phone. "They have a bed for you at Cedars. Tomorrow."

"Tomorrow?"

"Get there at six."

"Six in the morning?"

"Right," he says and rings off.

"I don't have any nice nightgowns," I turn and say to Billy.

Billy pretends this is a perfectly reasonable response.

Sally and I head for Nordstrom's at the Grove. We pass the chocolate counter just inside the entrance, ignoring the delicious aroma, and make our way through clouds of perfume from the cosmetic counters to the shoe department. There's a sale going on, and the place is swarming with Hollywood girls in tight minis and four-inch heels, their hair the colors of anything but hair. I watch them as they pull jewel-encrusted cell phones out of designer bags, a pack of cigarettes toppling to the floor, and wonder what lies ahead for them. *Forever* is what I suspect they would say.

It is what I would have said.

The little nodule in my neck turns out to be malignant, a miniscule expeditionary force (a mass of one billion cancer cells cannot be detected by even the most advanced medical equipment) that escaped the terrorist camp in my kidney and sneaked past the 20 trillion immune cells that were supposed to be keeping watch — Were they unarmed? Hadn't they had their broccoli that day? –- and made its way to the right supraclavicular lymph node inside the collar bone to set up a new camp. The new diagnosis was metastatic Transitional Cell Cancer. This puts me at Stage IV.

"Is there a Stage V?" I ask.

"No," the surgeon answers.

"I see."

I look over at Billy and Sally. They are standing quite still, their faces pale.

"Well then," I say. "We better fix it."

Since this type of high-grade TCC travels fast to the lungs, liver or bone, a new strategy is devised. We will systematically blast the cancer with medical weapons of mass destruction—top-of-the-line chemo—then, when I am sufficiently recovered from the chemo, remove the kidney.

This last part I did not hear. My mind had come to a halt at the mention of chemo. Every healer, shaman and medicine man I had ever known said the same thing: Once a person has had chemo, the body is too poisoned to receive healing.

I look at the faces of my children. Billy's eyes are fixed on me as if he is reading my thoughts.

When I was diagnosed with breast cancer 15 years ago, I said I was not going to have chemo. Bill and Billy ganged up on me, and I caved. I can blame that decision on them, or I can own up to my own lack of courage to follow the dictates of my beliefs. It's a runaway train, this cancer diagnosis, careening down a perilously steep hill. No way to put on the brakes and give myself time to think. I'm well into the Land of Cancer now.

Moments later, Anthony comes rushing into the hospital room and, sobbing, throws himself onto the bed. We have a code, he and I. Bill died wearing his favorite shirt, an orange fleece pullover which we kept on him during the days and nights we sat vigil at the funeral chapel.

"Don't you go chasing the orange shirt, Mama," Anthony warns. "Promise me."

He says it again now. "*Promise.*"

"I promise," I whisper.

At night, after everyone has gone and I am alone in the hospital room, dark now except for the ghastly yellow rectangle of light under the door, I do not take the pain pill or the sleeping pill. I am in no hurry for tomorrow. Instead I reach for my notebook and turn on the bedside lamp. I prefer to spend these precious hours in my other world:

I had left Peter and Sara in their hotel room in Rio having a terrible row. Peter had gone out and gotten paints and canvasses, and turned their room into a studio. For two whole days he painted furiously, never leaving the room. Following the midnight New Year's Eve ceremony during which he reluctantly accepted the cup of potion (which turned out to be cachaça blessed by the Black Pope), he discovers that he is painting in a mysteriously new way.

A feeling he did not recognize and could not describe. It started with a sense of profound calm, then after a moment a soft gentle warmth would envelope him and his mind would go completely blank. Then came the tingling sensation. It started at the back of his neck and flow down his arms into his hands to the tips of his fingers. All sense of time would disappear. He did not need food or sleep. Just this, he murmured. Just this…

On the third day, Sara came in with shopping bags and set them down. "Aren't you going to let me see them yet?" she asked, barely able to keep the exasperation out of her voice.

She'd been sightseeing and shopping alone, lunching alone, even dining alone in the hotel dining room.

"Yes, now I'm ready to show you." He stood aside. Sara stared, speechless. It was a woman in a long full skirt wading into the water, her arms filled with flowers. The hem of her dress was heavy, soaked, clinging to her legs. With just a few lines he managed to show the woman's expression. The colors were clear and vibrant, the brushstrokes sure. The oval faces were blank, featureless, yet full of life: the canvas exploded with emotion.

"Sara, look. See the flat, two-dimensional figures? And the colors – straight from the paint tubes – pure naïf, right?"

He showed her another, this one of the man he had told her about, the Black Pope, sitting on his throne in the sand holding a cup. He was grinning. Sara took a half step back. Again, with only the fewest lines, she could see something faintly unmistakably evil in the mouth. The tiny curve at the corners of the mouth. And the eyes. Peter had painted them flat black, yet... She felt a twinge of – what? Fear? She looked over at Peter. His face was flushed with excitement, his eyes so bright that for a brief moment she wondered if he had taken something.

She didn't know what to say. She took off her shoes and put them in the closet.

"You haven't told me yet. Do you like what I'm doing? You can tell me, you know," he said. "If you don't think it's working, tell me."

"It's just that it's so new for you. I have to get used to it."

"Yes it's new. We know that. But do you like it?"

"Peter, yes – yes, I think I do." She didn't mean it to come out sounding so weak.

"You think?"

"I mean it's so different…" Something about it frightened her. Something dark yet at the same time – what? – holy, in a strange way.

"New. Different." He threw his hands in the air. "C'mon. You can do better than that, can't you? You like it or you don't. Like, don't like. Good, bad. Yes, no. See, look outside. That's day. Tonight it will be dark. Night. Day, night. Sun, moon. It's easy."

"Stop it! Stop it!" she sobbed and ran into the bathroom and slammed the door.

But Peter was lost in the magic. I would escape to the magic if I dared. Before the magic turned away from me and was lost to me forever. At the bottom of the page I had scrawled: *You can't expect to go through the looking glass without getting cut.*

A nurse comes into the room and switches on the harsh, overhead light so suddenly that I raise my arms to shield my eyes. She takes my temperature, checks my blood pressure and asks if I need anything. I shake my head no. She insists that I take my pill and stands over me while I wash it down with water. I am on this side of the looking glass now, a captive in the Land of Cancer during the Moon of the Terrible. I drift into a dark, dreamless sleep to the sound of the wolves howling outside the door.

FEBRUARY - ICE MOON

As a new moon arrived, the Lakota
people noticed a great change.
Trees on the Great Plains popped
and burst as their branches became
laden with winter snow and ice.
The people huddled around the
fire listening to the stories
the Elders told.

(Lakota Sioux)

Huddled in winter under the February moon, chilly and damp even in Southern California, the family assembles around me as chemo treatments begin. Like the snow-laden branches of the trees on the Great Plains, my bones have turned to ice. I ask the doctors whether it's the disease that's making me so cold or the chemo. The oncologist says it's the disease, Keith Agre says it's the chemo. I think the cause of my deep chill is fear — of both the disease and the cure. I pile on sweaters as everyone else peels off theirs; we tighten the circle against the approaching storm.

To read more Buy *The Thirteenth Moon* from Amazon.com   [http://www.amazon.com/The-Thirteenth-Moon-Journey-Healing/dp/1453600078/ref=pd_sim_b_2]